An Introduction to Gender and Wellbeing in Microeconomics

An Introduction to Gender and Wellbeing in Microeconomics explains how to set up the basics of designing a gender-aware approach to microeconomics by constructing creative gender-aware indicators. In microeconomics, the economic decisions of individuals, households, communities, social groups, firms, businesses and entrepreneurs stand central to economic analysis.

Using a wellbeing economics framework, the book argues that economic models should take power differences such as those inherent with gender into account, and be complemented by more qualitative analysis geared to discovering the 'how' and 'why' behind the 'what' questions.

This book will be essential reading to academic and professional researchers, as well as policy researchers in the field of gender and economics, international development, social and economic policy. It will be invaluable for courses relating gender to the economy, and will enable readers to get a clear and concise understanding of the gendered character of the economy and of economic policy.

Nicky Pouw is an economist with over twenty years of research and teaching experience in the field of international development. She is affiliated as an Associate Professor within the Governance and Inclusive Development research programme at the University of Amsterdam in the Netherlands. She has done extensive research on poverty, inequality, human development, gender and wellbeing, mostly in African economies. From this applied, grounded research she has heuristically developed her own ideas on the epistemology of economics and inclusive development, on which she has published widely. Her comprehensive and gender-aware approach to economics has culminated out of many years of applied economic research, working and teaching in multi-disciplinary environments and being concerned most with seeing the economy from the perspective of ordinary people in relation to their living environment.

An Introduction to Gender and Wellbeing in Microeconomics

Nicky Pouw

LONDON AND NEW YORK

First published 2018
by Routledge
2 Park Square, Milton Park, Abingdon, Oxon, OX14 4RN

and by Routledge
711 Third Avenue, New York, NY 10017

Routledge is an imprint of the Taylor & Francis Group, an informa business

British Library Cataloguing-in-Publication Data
A catalogue record for this book is available from the British Library

Library of Congress Cataloging-in-Publication Data
A catalog record for this book has been requested

ISBN: 978-0-415-46183-2 (hbk)
ISBN: 978-1-315-73504-7 (ebk)

Typeset in Times New Roman

by diacriTech, Chennai

MIX
Paper from
responsible sources
FSC   FSC™ C013985
www.fsc.org

Printed in the United Kingdom
by Henry Ling Limited

to Eugène, Lulu, Eva & Rosa

to Eugene, Lulu, Elliot Boyd

Contents

Figures

Tables

Preface

The purpose of this book is to introduce a gender-aware and wellbeing approach to studying economic issues and phenomena, with an emphasis on economic problems of resource agents in the microeconomy. It is aimed at understanding the economy in a more comprehensive and balanced manner, taking into account both women's and men's performances, needs, priorities and power relations in the economy. As such, the book tries to overcome the inherent androcentric bias of the economic discipline, which has long been influencing gender-biased, market-oriented theories, concepts and methods. 'Homo-economicus' has served as a longstanding universal representation of people's role in the economy in general, but represented men's economic activities much more than women. This book is an attempt, therefore, to restore part of that imbalance found in microeconomic theories, concepts and methods and guide students and researchers in taking a more gender-aware approach.

Although, by now many scholars and practitioners recognize the importance of taking a gender-aware approach in economics, not many know precisely how to do it. The background and motivation of this book can be traced back to its early origins in feminist economic thought, but also to social and political economy and international development studies and their respective critiques of neoliberal or mainstream economics over the past decades. These fields are relatively open to pluralism, which provides an entry point for bringing power and culture into economics. Where on the one hand, feminist economics have emphasized the gender biases in economic structures, processes, policies, institutions and outcomes and the importance of taking power relations in multiple economic domains into account; on the other hand critical thinkers in the field of international development studies have been pertinent about cultural values and context-specific factors shaping the economy on the ground. In this book these two worlds meet-up and enabled me to give hands and feet to my vision of a gender-aware microeconomics. In doing so, my epistemological departure point is a wellbeing economics framework that Allister McGregor and I have been developing together. Our many conversations about 'what economics is all about' are a continuous source of inspiration, and will feed into a follow-up of this book on gender, wellbeing and macroeconomics.

Nicky Pouw
Amsterdam, 23 February 2017

Acknowledgements

The inception of this book dates back to my first introductions to economics at pre-university high school. Amongst calculus and mathematics, which I loved, and social sciences and languages, which where culturally attractive, economics was a strange and abstract topic for me. Maybe this was because economics and I started our long-term relationship from an initial misconception: I thought that economics was all about the question 'how do people (anywhere in the world) make a living (a question I always asked my parents on travels abroad), whereas the economics I was taught in school started out with explaining a macroeconomic formula of GDP. I found myself subsequently struggling to grasp what economics was really all about in subsequent years, and how that could be resolved with my own view on the economy and on economics as a discipline – in the early years of my study I hardly succeeded. I guess this made me determined to grasp economics better and acquire the necessary knowledge and skills to embark on a Master of Science and PhD in Economics in subsequent study phases.

Despite these initial set-backs, I gradually succeeded in finding my own way through economics and coming to terms on what the economy and the discipline was all about. On this journey I have been lucky to encounter many scholars and practitioners who were questioning and clarifying the purpose and scope of economics, like me, for multiple reasons. This gave me the space to think creatively – out-of-the-box – about economics, but also to trace its roots back in history to political economy and philosophy. One revealing angle I stumbled across was through feminist economics. In the late-1990s, as a student at the University of Amsterdam I was privileged to be taught by Siv Gustafsson on gender and economics, and be a student in the economics group in which Henriëtte Maassen-van den Brink, Edith Kuiper and Jolande Sap did their research. Through them I was invited to meetings with renowned scholars who were affiliated or visiting at the University of Amsterdam, including: Mary Morgan, Deidre McCloskey, Arjo Klamer, Irene van Staveren, Diane Elson, Nancy Folbre, and Susan Feiner. It was an exciting time during which the International Association for Feminist Economics (IAFFE) from the U.S. organized their annual conference in Amsterdam in 1995. Because of my deep interests in inequality and political relations, especially at the macroeconomic and international level, I specialized in development economics. In this field, I found the freedom to work in multidisciplinary teams on concrete human development problems. At the Institute of Social Studies (ISS) in The Hague I worked with Graham Pyatt, Lucia Hanmer and Howard White on participatory poverty assessments in Africa, and I was introduced to social accounting matrices on the side. Gender was always an important line of research within this poverty and development research. During that time, I also benefitted from working closely with Haroon Akram-Lodhi and Irene van Staveren. Their work in feminist development economics inspired me. I regret we could not write this book together. Both at ISS and the Free University in Amsterdam, where I completed my PhD with Jan Willem Gunning and Chris Elbers, I learned about the pro's and con's of econometric modeling approaches and techniques from design to application.

By Isa Baud and Johan Post I was invited to come to the University of Amsterdam and become part of the Governance and Inclusive Development research programme within the Amsterdam Institute of Social Science Research. Since I consider economics a social science this proved to be an appropriate place of work for me, and still is so today. Working with a broad range of multi-disciplinary scholars in the fields of international development studies and human geography, including Ton Dietz, Joyeeta Gupta, Dennis Arnold, Maarten Bavinck, Mirjam Ros-Tonen, Michaela Hordijk, Hebe Verrest, Mieke Lopes-Cardozo, Niels Beerepoot, Rive Jaffe, Courtney Vegelin, Yves van Leynseele, Esther Miedema, Winny Koster, and Joeri Scholtens enabled me to translate my bottom-up and heuristic ideas on economics, into clear epistemological and ontological ideas on economic knowledge. Furthermore, my intellectual exchanges with Ewald Engelen, in the same department, underlying mainstream economic thought encouraged me to think about a pluralist perspective in economics. At the same time, I always appreciated and kept my connection with economists at my home university and abroad, and within the Dutch and Foreign Ministries and Central Bureaus of Statistics. Engaging with economic practitioners made me very much aware of the performativity of economics as a discipline. In the meantime, an important conversation with Allister McGregor of Sheffield University evolved, out of a first meeting in India in 2012. His seminal writings on human wellbeing inspired me to redefine what economics to me is all about. Instead of the narrow conception of welfare, human wellbeing should feature centre stage I thought. I found Allister in agreement with me and together we developed an 'economics of wellbeing'. I am therefore indebted to all of these people for having inspired me and who helped shape my ideas in writing this book. Furthermore, I am grateful to my students in the International Development Studies programmes, Research Masters and MSc, at the University of Amsterdam, particularly to those in the Economics of Human Development course, for helping me test out some basic ideas and exercises in this book. I also thank my editor Emily Kindleysides and assistant editor Elanor Best for their skillful and patient guidance through the book writing process. I promise my second volume will be completed sooner than the first. Last but not least, I wish to especially thank my department head, Johan Post and research director Joyeeta Gupta for giving me time off from teaching to complete this book. Both the short-term article writing and longer-term, slow writing of a book are constitutive of what defines me as an academic. Ultimately, there is much more value in alteration and diversity than in mono-disciplinary tasks then most economic theories would predict.

1 Introduction

A gender-aware approach to the economy puts people at the centre of the economy. A people-centered economics takes concrete economic problems that people are confronted with in their daily lives as the starting point. The people who are engaged in solving economic problems based on multi-dimensional trade-offs are defined 'resource agents' in this book. Multi-dimensional trade-offs in wellbeing exist because resource agents exercise agency in multiple economic domains. Since economic problems are complex, a simple uni-dimensional framework does not suffice to study economic problems from multiple angles and interest points. This is where a more comprehensive framework such as the wellbeing economics framework developed by Allister McGregor and Nicky Pouw (2014, 2016) comes in to facilitate more complex analyses.

Moreover, most microeconomic models do not take power relations into account *a priori*. Yet, in considering gender inequalities in economic relations, policies, processes and outcomes, power plays a key role in shaping these. This is why economic models should take power differences and relationships into account, and be complemented by more qualitative analysis geared to discovering the 'how' and 'why' behind the 'what' questions. A gender-aware approach implies conducting gender analysis. This book explains how to set up the basics of designing gender-aware modeling approaches and construct gender-aware indicators creatively. Sometimes indicators are mistaken for facts, but indicators are constructs too and informed by theory and opinions.

In Chapter 2 it is explained why a gender-aware approach is important for understanding how resource agents make economic decisions. These decisions involve multiple trade-offs between their entangled resource agency in the paid and unpaid economy, and between different dimensions of wellbeing. The gender-aware approach of this book is embedded within a broader epistemological and theoretical framework of wellbeing economics. The recent progress made with wellbeing economics is linked to developments and critical debates in heterodox economics and international development studies, which propose a pluralist perspective in economics. Chapter 3 explains the basic principles of a wellbeing economics framework, as well as its underlying ontological and epistemological principles and axioms. The remaining chapters of this book address the different resource agents in the microeconomy, considering their economic wellbeing from a gender-aware perspective: individuals and households in Chapter 4, communities and social groups in Chapter 5, and firms, businesses and entrepreneurs in Chapter 6. The book ends with Chapter 7 on the need for a broader conceptualization of economic performance. The debate around economic performance, how we evaluate it and with the use of methods and metrics, spans the micro- and macroeconomy. It can therefore also be seen as pre-emptive thinking about a gender-aware approach to the macroeconomy.[1]

The chapters will introduce a set of key concepts and definitions to create a common understanding and build-up basic knowledge. Furthermore, the reader is invited to develop a fresh, gender-aware perspective on these concepts, and about the implications of this more comprehensive approach in terms of modeling relationships in the microeconomy. The theoretical models introduced are but a first step in thinking systematically and creatively about more specific, empirically informed models and relationships. As such, the models form a stepping stone into that direction, which would require a more technical and specialized exposition that is most suitable for any economist to learn, but beyond the scope of this book. The development of gender-aware indicators and policies will also be addressed in Chapters 3 to 7.

Each chapter concludes with a list of key learning points; these form a "red line" through the chapters. Moreover, each chapter includes a set of individual and group assignments and discussion points at the end. A tutor or lecturer can use this to deepen and test students/participants understanding and proficiency of the topics and methodologies explained. The exercises are flexible to re-design, elaboration, and tailoring to context-specific needs within various classroom or training settings. An important feature of this book is to create more room for creative thinking on economics, from a multiplicity of angles and disciplinary approaches. The exercises are designed to stimulate the creativity of students and readers who engage themselves with this fascinating study of economics.

Note

1   Volume II on a Gender-Aware Approach to Macroeconomics is currently in the making.

References and suggested further reading

Pouw, N.R.M. and J.A. McGregor (2014) An Economics of Wellbeing. What would economics look like if it were focused on Human Wellbeing? in *IDS Working Paper 436*, Sussex, England: Institute of Development Studies.

McGregor, J.A. and N.R.M. Pouw (2016) Towards an Economics of Wellbeing. *Cambridge Journal of Economics*, 24 October 2016. https://doi.org/10.1093/cje/bew044

2 What is gender-aware economics?

2.1 What is gender and why does it matter in economics?

This book explains how economic processes and outcomes are shaped by gender. It provides theoretical, conceptual and methodological explanations of a gender-aware economics by focusing on resource agents and economic problems in the microeconomy.

Gender refers to the socially constructed norms and behaviors of women and men, girls and boys that transcend the identities, roles and relationships performed. In order to make the concept of gender tangible in economic analysis, it is broken down into three dimensions: identity, roles and relationships. Every day, women and men make economic decisions that affect their current state of wellbeing and the wellbeing of people around them. Their decisions also have an impact on the natural environment. Women and men make economic decisions individually, collectively or they get decisions imposed upon them. In this book, we zoom in on multidimensional human wellbeing, which can be assessed in objective and subjective terms in line with McGregor (2004). The human wellbeing concept will be introduced in Chapter 3. Furthermore, in this book when we construct models of individual/household, social groups/communities and firm-level economic wellbeing the focus is in line with the Organisation for Economic Co-operation and Development (OECD; 2013). Economic wellbeing is also defined in Chapter 3, section 3.1.

Box 2.1 Gender

Gender is the socially constructed norms and behaviors of women and men, girls and boys that transcend the *identities, roles* and *relationships* performed.

Gender identity refers to what it means to be and act as a woman or a man, girl or boy within a particular social environment in a given time and place. Gender roles interact with these socially constructed identities and refer to the different tasks and activities, responsibilities and behaviors women and men are accustomed to and what is considered socially appropriate. Gender relationships are then the socially constructed interactions between (groups of) women and men, expressed in relationships of power, collaboration, friendship, affection, love, competition, domination, coercion and force, etc. Gender relationships are embedded and reproduced through society's formal and informal institutions, thus permeating institutional structures, laws, rules, norms, customs and traditions. Gender identity, roles and relationships are also co-constitutive of each other. This is why Judith Butler (2010) speaks of gender as being a performative social phenomenon that produces and reproduces itself all the time. Societal institutions, including economic institutions, can reproduce or deepen pre-existing gender inequalities if they are not gender-aware.

Box 2.2 Performativity of gender

Gender is a *performative* social phenomenon that produces and reproduces itself all the time within a given societal context and period of time.

Source: Butler (2010).

Gender intersects with caste, class, religion, race and ethnicity, but also interacts with age, social and marital status and personal characteristics. In places where women and men work, gender interacts with other social constructs, such as religion, class, race or ethnicity shaping the structures and dynamics of the workforce. These complex interactions between gender and other social constructs are not always clearly visible to an outsider. But once knowing the cultural values influencing such interactions, one can reveal them.

Gender-awareness in economics thus means to be informed and attentive to gender identity, roles and relationships. Furthermore, it implies as economic researcher to be attentive to how gender bias and dynamics can influence economic decisions, processes and outcomes and cause gender inequalities in wellbeing. Economic decisions made today have implications on the wellbeing of future generations. From the natural and physical resource bases people leave behind, wellbeing is determined for the future. There is a great global concern that despite todays' affluent societies, people live in deep poverty, face structural inequality and hardship, are discriminated against and excluded, dominated, oppressed and maltreated. Globalization has not and will not solve these structural inequalities by itself. It is true that some of the old divides have started to disappear, but others remain and new ones continuously appear. Certain deprivations and inequalities affect entire groups of people, leading to durable inequalities; in the words of Charles Tilly, 'across categories of: caste, class, religion, race, ethnicity, age and gender' (1999). Among those durable inequalities, gender inequality is one of the most universal and pervasive one; particularly, difficult political and economic circumstances women and girls tend to bear the brunt. There is a growing recognition that globalization and rising levels of gross domestic product (GDP) are not enough to effectively address structural gender inequalities. Moreover, there is a growing recognition that gender inequalities intersect with other social-cultural or political inequalities and oppression or marginalization, thus creating new forms of inequality in wellbeing.

Considering the more negative side of gender and the economy, we find women and girls more often than not pulling the short end of the stick compared to their male counterparts, especially in cultures where patriarchy rules and subversion is enforced. Women's economic status, their participation in the economy, and competitive positions and rewards are on average less than men's. This is considered 'on average', as the opposite can also be true. On the more positive side, we find women's economic status and participation having improved considerably over the past fifty years or so, at least in those societies where democracy and freedom are being respected. But these historical changes do not necessarily correspond with development of new gender-aware economic theory and methods *sine qua non*. Economic theories and methods are remarkably slow in capturing the changing face of the real-life economy. Following Diane Elson's (1991) and Marianne Ferber and Julie Nelson's (1993) seminal works on male bias in economic development, we have written this book more than twenty years later because of the old economic textbooks used in class are still the same. Edith Kuiper argued (2001) that economic theories and methods have been developed and applied from a one-sided, male view on the economy and what economics is and should be all about. For example, a key figure in economics, the economic agent, has long been ascribed a narrow set of male-biased characteristics that not many people in real life can actually relate to. Feminist economists, and later the behavioral economists have denounced this delimiting notion of a 'homo economicus', whom supposedly behaves perfectly rational in gender-neutral markets. Rationality in that sense refers to economic decision making by comparing relative prices on a one-dimensional scale. However, people weigh in other, non-market factors as well when making economic decisions. Previous experiences, emotions, benevolence, reciprocity, opportunity costs in the household domain, custom and belief, cultural values, and a sense of social justice may all weigh into the decision. This widening scope of what shapes economic decision-making is why, in this book, economic agents are referred to as resource agents (see Section 2.3).

2.2 Gender inequality

For most women and men, the market is not a gender-neutral place, because society is not gender-neutral. Productive resources may be inaccessible, jobs may be out of reach, a proper and just reward may be non-negotiable because of gender inequality. Moreover, women's and men's autonomy and dignity in the economy may be seriously compromised by social and political restrictions, and their freedom to speak, act or protest may be suppressed. Social and cultural customs and beliefs work as powerful instruments to exclude women and girls from certain economic domains or include them under unfavorable or precarious conditions in other economic domains (e.g. prostitution, child labor). Religious and political rules may be used to justify such practices and beliefs. In some societies, parents do not invest in the education of girls since the prospect of these girls is (early) marriage and motherhood. Gender inequality, in those cases, is institutionalized in formal and informal rules, customs and beliefs that limit women to participate in the economy as independent and free human beings. Although, the majority of women do undertake economic activities, it is often times to support their husband, father or brother in their productive activities or manage the household and take care of the family. In both cases, women's labor is considered 'free'. As a result, much of the unpaid labor of women goes unrecorded in national statistics. In societies where the majority of women do earn an income of their own, we still find too many women (and girls) occupying the lower echelons of the workforce, being underpaid, overworked, exploited or abused. Sometimes, the economic opportunities of women and girls are so confined or overruled by others, that their economic undertakings are truly risky, and threatening to their bodily integrity, health and life. In those circumstances only bad choices can be made.

Box 2.3 Gender inequality

> An inequality in a process or outcome indicator between women and men (girls and boys) that is embedded within unequal power relations and reproduced by gendered norms and behaviors through societal institutions.

Unfortunately, the same can be said for many men and boys facing similar hardships and forms of injustice. We need to also keep an open view to gender inequalities potentially working the other way round. Finally, in addressing gender issues in the economy it should be clear that although we speak of 'women' and 'men', they are not homogenous categories. It is our aim to consider women's and girls' experiences in the economy in all their diversity, heterogeneity and complexity. A gender-aware economics can help to make gender inequalities visible, measurable and targetable.

2.3 The paid and unpaid economy

An important analytical distinction made throughout this book is between the paid and unpaid economy. The paid economy refers to the corporative and public domain of the economy in which goods and services are produced in return for payment – this includes the formal and informal economy (including the subsistence, or barter economy), and the state that provides (subsidized) goods and services to its citizens and firms. The unpaid economy refers to the private domain of the economy of households and social groups, communities and neighborhoods, where valuable goods and services are produced for free by means of household or voluntary work. Although, no price is attached to the production of such goods and services, they are not without costs. There are opportunity costs, also called 'foregone earnings, attached to producing unpaid goods and services. The paid and unpaid economy is interconnected as well as interdependent. In fact, when we speak of 'the economy', we refer to the paid and unpaid economy as one whole, representing two sides of the same coin – see Figure 2.1.

One of the red lines through this book is the idea that in most present-day societies the paid economy cannot function without the unpaid economy, and *vice versa*. The barter economy, as a society-wide economic system in which goods and services are directly exchanged for other goods and services without market mediation, is an exception but has become increasingly marginal. As new (and not so new) phenomena, we do come across economic initiatives in small sub-sectors of the economy that are being organized along barter-economy principles, or contain

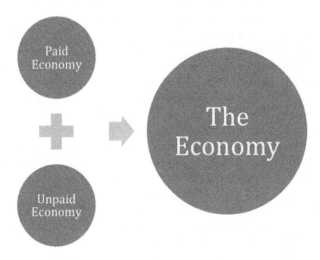

Figure 2.1 The paid and unpaid economy together make up the economy.

elements thereof.[1] The paid and unpaid economy can be thought of as two communicating vessels as far as economic agents, spaces where production and consumption take place, and substitutable goods and services are concerned. For example, when there is a budget cut in childcare services being subsidized by the public sector, we observe agents in the unpaid economy taking over the provision of childcare. Vice versa, if the unpaid economy produces more voluntary services to community members and social groups (for example, house repair, cooking meals for others), the paid economy may be circumvented. If the unpaid economy were entirely self-sufficient, it could function without the paid economy. Where this used to be the case for subsistence economies long time ago, it is becoming a rare phenomenon nowadays.

But it is equally difficult to imagine the paid economy functioning without the labor (people), spaces, goods and services (re)produced and regenerated in the unpaid economy. The paid and unpaid economy are thus inter-connected in multiple ways. Decisions made in one domain, affect the other at multiple levels (international, macro, micro). Yet, in many economic models the paid and unpaid economy are separated and their multi-level inter-connections remain under-studied. A gender-aware economics can help to bridge these old divides and better understand economic decision-making from such an integrated perspective.

The majority of women worldwide actively participate in the paid economy to earn an income, yet they do not always face the circumstances, opportunities and constraints that men do. Partly, these conditions are created within the paid economy itself: the types of jobs available for women and men may be different due to differences in the accumulated human capital by women and men. These conditions are also partly influenced by the 'performance' of gender in the unpaid economy and wider society. Judith Butler (1999) defined gender performativity as the ways in which gender identities, roles and relationships play out in reiterated acts of women and men, whilst obscuring their personal singularities and contradictions. These acts lead to gender narratives and certain ways of questioning or reasoning human behavior. "Who pays for the kids?" is one of those questions that Nancy Folbre (1999) put forward, which can be answered by different stereo-type gender narratives; men pay for the kids because they are breadwinner of the family, or women pay because of their unpaid (and undervalued) household and caretaking work. As a full-time working mother of three, people often ask me how I get things organized at home? The question is posed to me more frequently than to my husband, who is also a full-time working parent. Some people ask me how *we* get things organized at home, but usually they ask how *I* get it organized, as if I were solely responsible. When I add that I am travelling abroad for my work on a regular basis, some people frown. If my husband states he is travelling, the reactions are generally more positive and enthusiastic. Gender performativity is not always visible on the surface. It is deeply rooted in gendered norms, culture and codes of conduct, and this ultimately influences the way we behave personally and in relation to our environment.

Economic decisions, institutions, processes and policies are also influenced by gender; although societies and individuals clearly differ in the extent to which they impose social norms upon others. A gender-aware economics aims to reveal the intrinsic gender inequalities embedded and reproduced by economic decisions, institutions, processes and policies, by raising awareness. Moreover, a gender-aware economics suggests new ways of thinking and organizing the economy in a more gender-equal manner by doing justice to women's and men's dignity and autonomy as equal human beings. Although we contend that gender can be a sticky matter that can be firmly enclosed in social practices and institutions, it is not completely fixed. Gender is, like any other social phenomenon, subject to continuous adaptation, contestation, re-negotiation, and transformation.

2.4 Picturing the economy and basic economic concepts

Many economic theories and methods have been constructed in the past on the basic premises of the 'market economy' only. This market, where buyers and sellers exchange goods and services, were assumed to be neutral. The outcome of the exchange process depended on relative prices only, and was independent of someone's race, gender, age, class, ethnicity or religion. In this book we assert that markets are not neutral by definition – specifically, we develop arguments against the perceived gender neutrality of markets and the economy as a whole. Instead, we argue that markets are embedded within a constellation of social and political institutions, and likewise, the economy as a whole is embedded in social and political institutions. Both have become construed within a natural environment. As a result of this embedding, the economic processes, policies and institutions themselves stand subject to cultural influences, power relations and natural change, as well as to the history of that. This is not to say that the economy is at the center of everything – but merely to say that the economy is central to the study of economics. We cannot think about the economy standing in isolation of the political, social and natural.[2]

Economic problems arise in the paid and unpaid domains of the economy, because decisions around the allocation of resources need to be made in both domains. This is not a new idea. Already in 1930, Margaret Reid argued that the household is a site of consumption as well as production. She referred to the household as the 'home economy'. Nowadays, the term 'care economy' is often used to denote the same thing. People in households make decisions about the allocation of resources on a daily basis. For example, when family members decide how to best use their limited time to clean the house, take leisure or spend more hours on a paid job; or, when a subsistence farmer decides what crops to grow on his/her plot of land; or, when a group of households in a neighborhood decides to invest money and time and volunteer to maintain the neighborhood park and playground. As a matter of fact, when people in households, communities and social groups make such decisions, these decisions have implications for the use of resources in the paid domain of the economy. Some resources (but not all) are scarce resources, and can only be used once (e.g. food). Some resources are scarce to everyone (e.g. time), whereas other resources are scarce to some, but not to others (e.g. living space or money). Economic decision making is not restricted to scarcity problems only. It also concerns allocative decisions regarding common pool resources. Resolving an economic problem in one economic domain (e.g. the household) has repercussions to people and resources in the same and other domains (e.g. the community, private sector). But also, an economic decision at the -level has implications for economic problems at the microlevel, and vice versa. These decisions can lie in the past, present or future. This makes economic problems complex, multi-dimensional and multi-layered. An economic problem that is reduced to a relative price dimension only is an abstraction from reality that can help to shed light on the monetary trade-off, while leaving other trade-offs in the dark.

Box 2.4 Economic problem

> An economic problem arises when a decision needs to be made with regard to the allocation of resources. Economic problems are complex, multi-dimensional and multi-layered.

Resource allocation thus does not only take place in the market (private sector), but also in the public sector and unpaid domain of households and communities/social groups. In Figure 2.2 the paid and unpaid economy are depicted separately from each other, although they are in fact two sides of the same coin (see also Figure 2.1). The two domains are interconnected and interdependent through the resources, activities and outcomes generated by people in the economy – embodied by individual women and men. People *are* the actors and form part of institutions in the paid and unpaid economy simultaneously. As a father and husband, one man may be member of a household, living in a small-town community, at the same time he may work as a government officer in the

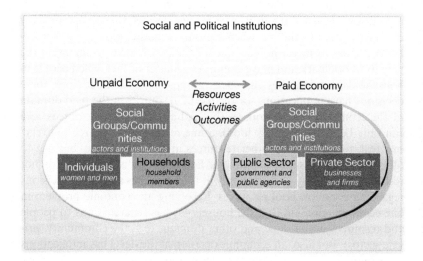

Figure 2.2 The instituted economy.

health ministry, and volunteer as a hockey-team trainer during his free time. As such, people resolve complex economic decisions about how to use resources in different life domains simultaneously.[3]

Resource agents are involved in solving an economic problem based on multi-dimensional trade-offs in wellbeing. Since resource agents exercise agency (or lack agency in disempowered situations) in multiple economic domains, these multi-dimensional trade-offs present themselves. In Chapter 3, it is further explained how and what complex trade-offs are made.

Box 2.5 Resource agents

Resource agents are involved in solving economic problems based on multi-dimensional trade-offs. Multi-dimensional trade-offs in wellbeing exist because resource agents exercise agency in multiple economic domains.

A further complexity is by seeing the economy as multi-layered, meaning that the allocation of scarce resources decided upon at one level of aggregation, has implications for scarce resource availability and use at other levels of aggregation. For example, if one individual farmer aims to increase her/his crop produce from one year to the next by increasing the use of chemical fertilizers on the land, this may worsen groundwater quality for other farmers not using fertilizers and diminishing total crop production of all the farmers. Likewise, private and public sector actors and institutions exercise agency at multiple levels of the economy, from micro to meso, macro and international.[4]

A last explanation in relation to Figure 2.2 is that the economy as a whole is embedded within a political and social institutional environment. This notion of the instituted economy will be explained in more detail in Chapter 3. For now, it suffices to present the economy as being embedded in a broader set of social and political institutions. Because of the instituted economy, economic agents themselves are seen to be influenced by social and political institutions.

2.5 The need for gender-responsive economic policy

National governments, to varying degrees, are seen by their constituencies to carry prime responsibility for social and economic policy-making in their country. Apart from the government, the private sector plays an important role in setting and influencing social, political and economic policies. Last, but not least, social groups and communities issue rules and regulations, norms and codes of conduct, and modes of cooperation, and may pressurize governments and private sector whilst also making their own (grassroots) arrangements that determine living conditions of women and men. For example, in a rural village in Burkina Faso it is common for people to organize a fundraising to pay collectively for the funeral and support of the family of the deceased if it concerns a poor family.

Box 2.6 Gender bias

> The differential treatment of individual women and men, girls or boys, or groups in society based on assumptions, beliefs and normative rules about their gender.

Many social and economic policies, measures and civic arrangements suffer from gender-blindness. Gender-blindness refers to the oversight of gender identities, roles and relationships that cause gender biases to occur in economic policy processes and outcomes. Amartya Sen, philosopher and economist, counted "more than 100 million women missing" (Sen 1990: p. 62) worldwide (in the early 1990s) due to heavily biased mortality rates among women and girls in developing countries. Often, social and economic policies are acclaimed to be gender-neutral, whereas in fact they are gender-blind (Elson 1991, 1995; Pouw 1995). Despite good intentions, many policies therefore do not achieve the desired objective, for example, the objective of equal girls and boys completion rate in secondary schools by making secondary schooling free of charge for every kid. However, providing equal funds to secondary schooling of girls and boys, does not guarantee equal completion rates in societies, where girls' dropout rates are higher than boys due to early pregnancies and marriages.

The opposite of a gender-blind policy is gender-responsive policy. A gender-responsive economic policy takes into account that gender identities, roles and relationships exist and can cause gender-biases in economic policy processes and outcomes. A gender-responsive economic policy seeks to address the differential situations, needs and interests of women (UNDP 2012), and men, girls and boys, but also tries to identify situations and conditions in which women and men collaborate and are mutually supportive. In the example of secondary schooling above, a gender-responsive policy could imply the decision to spend extra funding and effort on changing attitudes and behaviors among female and male adults and children in- and outside of school regarding sexual relationships and early marriage practices, instead of complementing the policy to abolish school fees.

Box 2.7 Gender responsive economic policy

> A gender responsive policy takes into account that gender identities, roles and relationships exist and may cause gender-biases in economic policy process and outcome. It addresses gender-specific situations, needs and interests of women and men, girls and boys and aims to undo gender inequalities.

Before being able to formulate and implement gender-responsive policies, there is the need to conduct an in-depth gender-aware analysis of the economic problem at hand.

What guides a gender-aware analysis of economic problems is:

1 Gender-aware research questions
2 Gender-aware methods and tools
3 Gender data and indicators
4 Gender-aware monitoring and evaluating instruments

Gender-aware questions are important to ask for understanding what gender inequalities in the economy prevail within a given context and time. Gender-aware methods and tools are then needed to reveal the underlying mechanisms that cause gender inequalities in the economy to persist, and how these are inter-linked with other social-economic and political factors and phenomena. Gender data is needed to assess the nature and size of the gender inequality concerned and construct gender indicators. Gender indicators are useful to inform and evaluate social and economic policies, and monitor changes over time. They provide a potentially powerful set of tools in the hands of analysts and policymakers to identify gender-sensitive objectives and formulate gender-responsive policies, and convince others to do the same. A gender-sensitive objective can focus on enhancing efficiency, equal opportunities, or equity in the achieved outcomes.

Before implementing a gender-responsive policy, the following steps need to be taken:

Step 1 – Specify the gender-sensitive objectives of the policy. What is it that you want to achieve? And especially, is it is efficiency-, equality- or equity-oriented?
Step 2 – Examine the current situation and nature of the economic problem signaled from different angles and perspectives, including a gender-aware perspective.

Step 3 – Define and collect the data needed to construct gender indicators to be used to achieve the stated objectives, within the available budget and time.

Step 4 – Explore the different policy options and scenarios and predict their gender impact by using the gender indicators defined.

Step 5 – Identify appropriate gender-aware monitoring and evaluating instruments, as well as key moments for feedback and policy adjustment, during and after policy implementation.

In designing a gender-responsive economic policy, analysts and policymakers should distinguish between responding to shorter term, practical gender needs to resolve; and economic problem and longer-term, strategic gender needs addressing the performativity of gender. Caroline Moser (1993) suggested such a distinction to be useful for making decisions about development funds. Strategic gender needs typically involve awareness-raising, attitudinal and institutional changes to become free of gender bias. These take much longer time than most policy budget cycles, and need to be considered in relation to other public dialogues and debates. Practical gender needs involve the removal of immediate constraints or fulfillment of shorter-term needs arising out of women's and men's performed gender identities, roles and relationships.

Box 2.8 Practical and strategic gender needs

- Practical gender needs refer to the practical, daily needs of women and men, girls an boys arising out of their performed gender identities, roles and relationships.
- Strategic gender needs refer to the longer-term awareness-raising, attitudinal and institutional changes to overcome gender bias.

Source: Caroline Moser (1993).

2.6 Learning points

- Gender refers to the socially constructed norms and behaviors of women and men, girls and boys that transcend the identities, roles and relationships performed.
- Gender performativity means that gender is a social phenomenon that produces and reproduces itself all the time within a given societal context and period of time.
- The paid and unpaid economy together make-up the economy. The two are inter-related and inter-dependent.

• Economic theories and methods in the past were built on assumptions of rational economic agency and gender-neutral markets.
• Economic problems are complex, multi-dimensional and multi-layered. Resource agents are engaged in solving economic problems by making multi-dimensional trade-offs.
• A gender-responsive economic policy aims to reveal gender biases in processes and institutions and counter gender inequality in the economy by means of addressing practical and strategic gender needs.

2.7 Assignments and discussion points

Assignment 1 – Draw a picture of yourself in the economy
Distribute a handout on which **Figure 2.1 – The paid and unpaid economy together make up the economy** – is printed. Ask students to draw in where they see themselves in the economy. Students may find themselves as resource agents in multiple domains at the same time. Ask them to write down what economic problems they encounter in which domains.

Assignment 2 – Getting girls to complete primary school
Work in small groups of 4–5 students. Assign the following group roles: (i) Kiballe District Commission on Gender (DCG) in Uganda (ii) Parents of schoolchildren (iii) School Board (iv) Local farmers and entrepreneurs. The DCG has stated as its objective to have 50% of the girls completing advanced primary level in five years time, and 100% in ten years time. What can different actors do to address the obstacles and constraints faced by girls to enroll and complete primary school until the advanced level? Each group prepares at least one statement and one action point. These will be presented in a role-play whereby the DCG calls all groups to a public hearing. Given the DCG's limited resources, only two ideas can be adopted.

Discussion point 1 – Production in the paid and unpaid economy (15 minutes)
Students team-up with their immediate neighbor to discuss for five minutes what production activities take place in the paid economy, and by whom. List all activities in one column. Spend another five minutes discussing what production activities take place in the unpaid economy. List these activities in a column next to the first column. Spend the last five minutes discussing how production activities in the paid and unpaid economy are inter-related – draw arrows between connected activities. The teacher can take extra time for the teams to present to the group.

Discussion point 2 – Gender inequalities in the economy (10–15 minutes)
Organize a plenary discussion on what examples of gender inequalities
students can think of in their own country, and abroad. Ask what policies and measures students know of that have been taken to address
gender inequalities. Were these policies and measures successful? Why/
why not?

Notes

1 These initiatives are further discussed in Chapter 6.
2 This notion of the economy as 'instituted' and an open system is further
   explained in Chapter 3 on the Wellbeing Economics Framework.
3 For this reason, in Chapter 3 the concept of 'entangled agency' is explained
   (see Section 3.2) to signify the conflation of agency.
4 These multiple levels of the economy are further explained in Chapter 3.

References and suggested further reading

Butler, J. (1999) *Gender Trouble: Feminism and the subversion of identity*, New
   York, NY: Routledge.
Butler, J. (2010) Performative agency, *Journal of Cultural Economy*, *3*(2): 147–161.
Elson, D. (1991) *Male Bias in the Development Process*, Manchester, UK:
   Manchester University Press.
_____ (1995) Gender awareness in modeling structural adjustment, *World
   Development*, *23*(11): 1851–1868.
Ferber, M. and Nelson J. (eds.) (1993) *Beyond Economic Man Feminist Theory
   and Economics*, Chicago: The University of Chicago Press.
Folbre, N. (1999) *Who Pays for the Kids?* London, UK: Routledge.
Kuiper, E. (2001) *The Most Valuable of all Capital. A Gender Reading of Economic
   Texts*, Amsterdam, NL: Thela Thesis.
McGregor, J.A. (2004) Researching wellbeing: Communicating between the needs
   of policy makers and the needs of people, *Global Social Policy*, *4*(3): 337–358.
Moser, C. (1993) *Gender Planning and Development. Theory, Practice and
   Training*, London, UK: Routledge.
OECD (2013) OECD Framework for Statistics on the Distribution of Household
   Income, Consumption and Wealth, Paris: OECD.
Pouw, N.R.M. (1995). Gender relations in the development process. *A Theoretical
   Analysis of the World Bank's Economic Framework*. Amsterdam: Publisher of
   doctoral thesis: University of Amsterdam.
Pouw, N.R.M. (1998). *Home Economics: Developing an Alternative Perspective*.
   Brussels: Women in Development Europe (WIDE).
Reid, M.G. (1930) *The Economics of Household Production*, New York, NY:
   John Wiley & Sons.
_____ (1938) *Consumers and the Market. Getting and Spending*, New York, NY:
   Arno Press.
Sen, A. (1989) Women's survival as a development problem, *Bulletin of the
   American Academy of Arts and Sciences*, *43*(2): 14–29.

Sen, A. (1990). More than 100 million women are missing. The New York Review of Books, 37(20), 61–66.

_____ (1990a) Gender and cooperative conflict, in Irene Tinker (ed.) *Persistent Inequalities – Women and World Development*, New York, NY: Oxford University Press, pp. 123–149.

_____ (1990b) More than 100 Million Women are Missing, *The New York Review of Books*, December 20.

_____ (1992) Missing women, *British Medical Journal*, 304(6827): 586-587.

Tilly, C. (1999) *Durable Inequality*, Berkeley: University of California Press.

3   Wellbeing economics framework

with Allister McGregor

3.1 Human wellbeing at the centre of economics

A wellbeing economics serves as the overarching framework to guide the gender-aware economic approach in this book. The epistemological contention behind the wellbeing economics framework is a more comprehensive vision of the economy. The central thesis being that the economy is more than just about money and markets, but rather a social phenomenon with human wellbeing as its prime concern. Human wellbeing is defined, according to Allister McGregor (2004, 2007), in terms of what people have in material sense, how they are able to use what they have in relational sense, and the level of satisfaction or subjective quality of life derived from this. Human wellbeing is thus not only about what one can achieve as an individual by maximizing self-interest (even though this can include others), but in relation to others and the environment, and whilst making multiple trade-offs. The human being as a *social* human being thus replaces the rational economic agent theory in neoclassical economics.

Box 3.1 Human wellbeing

> Human wellbeing theory distinguishes between three inter-related dimensions — material, social-relational and subjective wellbeing — what people have in material sense, how they are able to use what they have in relational sense, and the level of satisfaction or subjective quality of life derived from this.

Source: McGregor (2007)

Building on this notion of making human wellbeing a prime concern of economics, the economy is not a closed system consisting of fixed parameters and functioning by self-regulation.[1] Ultimately, it is people themselves, and not some kind of 'invisible hand' at the center of the economy steering economic processes and outcomes in order to protect, sustain or enhance their human wellbeing. This human strive for continuous improvement of wellbeing is visualized in Figure 3.1 below. We will focus in particular on economic wellbeing when constructing models of individual/household, social groups/communities and firm-level economic wellbeing in subsequent chapters. Economic wellbeing specifically refers to the command over resources and relations, and the satisfaction thereof. Economic wellbeing, like human wellbeing, is thus three-dimensional. But economic wellbeing is a slightly narrower concept than human wellbeing, which also entails resources and relations that cannot be commanded (e.g. people's relationship to time is more or less a given). If people's command over resources and relations is adequate relative to their needs and wants, we speak of economic *wellbeing*. If people's command over resources and relations is inadequate, we speak of economic *illbeing*. Negative manifestations of material, relational and subjective deprivation and illbeing are equally important to mention as part of this framework.

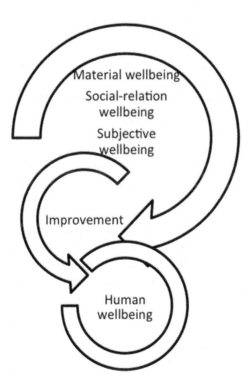

Figure 3.1 The continuous strive for the improvement of human wellbeing.

Box 3.2 Economic wellbeing

> People's command over resources and relations and satisfaction with
> quality of life. Economic wellbeing implies the command over resources
> and relations to be adequate relative to people's needs and wants.
> Economic illbeing implies an inadequate command or deprivation in one
> or more dimensions of wellbeing.

3.2 The economy as a social process

Much in line with Tony Lawson's (1997, 2003, 2015) critical writings
on the economics discipline being too far removed from people's daily
realities on the ground, the economy in the wellbeing framework is characterized as a social process because it is:

   I an instituted process;
  II an open system;
 III structured and layered;
 IV characterised by internal relations; and
  V having emergent properties.

These properties are explained one by one in the sections below.

3.2.1 The economy as an instituted process of resource allocation

The first premise is that the economy is an instituted social process. Such
a view is rooted in the seminal works of the economic historian Karl
Polanyi (1944) and later heterodox economists, including Tony Lawson,
Edward Fullbrook, John Davis, Ben Fine, Edith Kuiper, Frederic Lee,
Mark Lutz and Irene van Staveren. Following to their ideas, in this book
the economy is defined as the instituted process of resource allocation.
Institutions comprise the formal and informal rules and norms that
organize social, political and economic relations (North, 1990). The
economy is embedded within a political system, which itself is set within
a context- and time-specific social environment. Societies are embedded
within a particular natural and built environment, to which it is more

Box 3.3 The economy

> The economy is the instituted process of resource allocation. The economy
> is socially constructed and dynamic over time and place.

Source: McGregor and Pouw (2016)

or less closely related. As such, the economy is subject to social and political norms and values and to change over time.

This instituted view of the economy is represented in by means of four nested circles (see Figure 3.2). The sizes of the circles can change, vis-à-vis each other. The entry point of economic analysis constitutes always an economic problem; which is why 'economy' is represented as the inner circle here.

The nature of economic problems and the possible range of solutions are thus shaped by a broader economic, political, social-cultural and natural environment. Economic agents are engaged in solving economic problems in relationship to this complex environment. Defining the economy as the instituted process of resource allocation also creates space for making power differences between resource agents explicit. In doing economic analysis it allows one to explore how economic decisions are informed by people's position in society and sphere of influence,

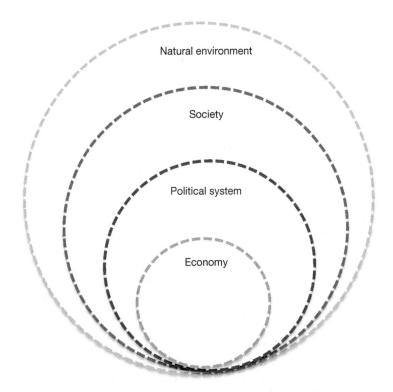

Figure 3.2 The economy embedded in a natural, social and political environment.

sense of identity, and relationship to one's economic, political, social and natural environment.

3.2.2 The economy as an open system

From the perspective of the economy as an instituted process of resource allocation, it is subsequently acknowledged that power relations between resource agents operate at all levels. Some of these relationships are embodied in codified laws, rules and institutions and others are more deeply embedded in cultural values, norms, customs and beliefs – as explained by Tony Lawson (1997, 2003). The economy is thus an open system that is influenced by 'exogenous' forces, including social-cultural, political and environmental conditions and changes. In this view resource exchange between agents is driven not only by relative prices within the narrowly defined economic system, but by a wider range of forces 'outside' the economy. These forces include political differences in resource and market access and control; people's culture and social habits; legal rules about factor payment; and concerns about the relationship between the natural environment and production and consumption processes. *Vice versa*, the economy also exercises force on the political, social and natural environment. In open systems, such as the economy, forces play out in both directions. This is why the circles in Figure 3.2 are dashed and not closed.

3.2.3 The economy as structured and layered

The economy is structured and layered in the same way as broader social processes are structured and layered. Economic structure refers to the way in which the economy is organized around its resource agents, institutions and sectors at multiple levels. This organization is temporal and subject to (long-term) change over time. Nevertheless, economic accounting and planning models are organized around these structures and layers. Once accepted, these models have a tendency to stay in use for long periods of time. This is because they become institutionalised in modes of work, methods and statistics, and formal institutions. For example, the United Nations international System of National Accounts (SNA) adopts the categories, structures and layers that are recognized in the economy at a certain moment in time and draws boundaries between them. It is an important economic planning tool to measure the total sum of resource flows in the economy. The SNA has been around since 1953, with marginal changes adopted slowly over time.

Economic categories, structures and layers also differ between types of economies and societies. In most political economic systems, there is

Box 3.4 Economic structure

Economic structure refers to the way in which the economy is organized around its various resource agents, institutions and sectors. The economy is multi-layered at the micro-, meso-, macrolevels, as well as the international level.

Source: McGregor and Pouw (2016)

a distinction made between the private and public sector. The private sector encompasses all for profit businesses of private persons and organizations that are not government owned. The public sector comprises all organizations owned and operated by the government, which provide goods and services for citizens, often times including basic goods and services such as drinking water, electricity, security, education and heath care. The composition of the private and public sector varies across countries. Another, more abstract categorization of the economy is into the paid and unpaid economy (as explained in Chapter 1, Section 1.3).

Economic categories are a useful starting point of economic analysis, but behind these categorizations is always a subjective choice.[2] Within the economy, the production, consumption and exchange of economic goods and services takes place at multiple levels of aggregation: micro, meso and macro: at the micro-level of the economy, individuals, households, communities and social groups (e.g. volunteer associations, sportclubs), businesses and firms exchange resources; at the mesolevel, economic structures mediate microlevel exchange and aggregate, macrolevel economic performance, (e.g. unemployment, growth, volatility, inequality, sustainability, and wellbeing); and at the international level, multi-lateral institutions, multi- and trans-national companies, and international non-governmental organisation (NGOs) (e.g. Red Cross) or community-based organisations (CBOs) (e.g. Slum Dwellers International) act as resource agents in the global economy.

3.2.4 The economy is characterised by internal relations

The economy is internally related through resource agents and resource flows. They use the following allocative mechanisms to organize exchange:

1 individuals, households and communities/social groups → reciprocity and mutual support (flourish, aspire, strive according to individual and shared life goals)
2 private sector (national and international firms) → market exchange (live well, live better by providing opportunities to improve wellbeing)

3 public sector (national and international government) →
   redistribution (live well together by sharing wellbeing)
4 Public Private Partnerships (PPPs) → hybrid allocation (combining
   any two of the above three)

It should be noted though, that apart from the three represented mechanisms in Figure 3.3 there also exist mechanisms of coercion, extortion, abuse and outright mischief that determine how resources are allocated. Those are examples of involuntary or oppressive mechanisms of resource allocation, which can be practiced by entire cultures or generations. Slavery, caste discrimination, racism and women's discrimination are examples in case. Inherently, these are unsustainable mechanisms due to their destructive outcomes on resources and agents, and the relations between them, which can nevertheless remain to exist for a long time.

In the unpaid economic domain, individuals, households and social groups/communities exchange resources with each other, such as time, food, space, goods and caring services, on the basis of the reciprocity principle, or mutual support. Reciprocity implies the exchange of a good or

Figure 3.3 Three driving mechanisms of resource allocation in the economy.

service for another good or service, as a positive reward to a kind action. A reward may be given in the present or future. For example, parents provide quality time with their kids in return for their love and affection, and/ or in return for the future care of the parents when they reach old age. Although, love and affection are not scarce, the time and money devoted to childcare are scarce. Mutual support implies the provisioning of goods and services in support of someone else, or something else like a social cause or voluntary activity, like working as trainer over the weekends at the local football club. Mutual support is given without the expectation that this act will be rewarded – although, the act in itself may be rewarding to the giver in another way (e.g. socially, mentally or spiritually). Reciprocity and mutual support can be perceived as positive or negative. For example, because of reciprocity family members may feel supported and strong, but reciprocity can also lead to high expectations and pressure that can feel like a burden to the family caretaker. Reciprocity and mutual support are not the only driving mechanisms of economic behavior in the unpaid domain.

In the paid economic domain of the the private sector, market exchange is the dominant allocation mechanism where resource allocation takes place. The market is a physical or non-physical space where exchange of goods and services between economic agents takes place. The price of a good or service is determined by supply and demand in the market. If supply of a particular good or service is high relative to demand, the price will be low. If demand of the good or service is high relative to supply, then the price will be high. Money facilitates impersonal market exchange between economic agents. However, not all market exchange is impersonal. A lot of market exchange is grounded in personal or business (e.g. brand community) relationships. In a few places worldwide, a traditional barter system of exchange is upheld, whereby economic agents exchange goods and services without the involvement of money. Barter economies, or bits and pieces of it, can still be found in rural economies, often as part of a bigger monetized economy. However, new systems of bartering are also coming and going in current times as a purposeful way to 'circumvent' the market. The latter will be a topic of discussion in Chapter 6.

Finally, in the paid economic domain of the public sector, the prime mechanism driving resource allocation is redistribution. Local and national governments collect taxes and earn income or interest from assets, that is being used to redistribute public goods and services in the economy, both in the unpaid and paid domain. For instance, a national government may wish to promote exports abroad by paying an export subsidy to chicken farmers, as is done in the US, Brazil and many European countries. Another example is the public provisioning of education and medical health care for free, or at starkly reduced rates. Redistribution can have an equalizing effect between individuals and households in the economy, since public goods and services are provided at below market prices. In this way, these goods and services become more affordable to people, irrespective of their income. Likewise, public goods and services may be provided in locations where the private companies do not want to invest because of high entry-costs, e.g. providing electricity and bus services in remote areas.

3.2.5 The economy has emergent properties

The objective of economic analysis is often prediction. An economics of wellbeing requires different metrics to play a role in analysing economic performance[3] providing the possibility of exploring different objectives (differing purposeful behaviours) and different values. There is not one criterion that can predict economic outcomes; there may be multiple criteria that apply to different sub-groups in society. This leads at best to scenario-based thinking, rather than single-point predictions. The economy has emergent properties when aggregating multi-dimensional wellbeing from the individual to the macrolevel. The very nature of economic relationships can change in this aggregation process, but they can also change over time because of uncertainty and shocks. The current methodological challenge for economists is to think about standard models and identify (new) feedback loops, explain anticipating behaviour of heterogeneous resource agents, and find ways to deal with multi-dimensional risk and uncertainties. Entangled agency is therefore introduced here as a concept reflecting the complexity of resource agents who are making multi-dimensional wellbeing decisions simultaneously, all the time. Complex economic decisions are made by making multiple trade-offs between:

I   different dimensions of wellbeing
II   individual and collective wellbeing
III   wellbeing over time

This is visually represented by the Venn diagrams in Figure 3.4 below. A Venn diagram is a useful first step for thinking logically about an economic problem and identifying people's priorities and needs. The three dimensions of wellbeing can be analytically considered as different sets. This is the first step in logically thinking about all possible relationships between the elements of the represented sets.

Figure 3.4 visualizes that people may put different emphasis on different dimensions of their wellbeing. Some people may prioritize the

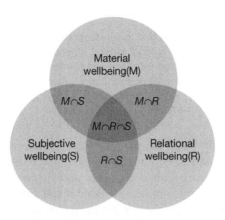

Figure 3.4 The three domains of wellbeing intersecting.

pursuit of their wellbeing primarily by means of material wellbeing *(M)*, but at the expense of their relational *(R)* and subjective wellbeing *(S)*. Alternatively, others may either choose, or be forced by circumstance, to downplay the fulfillment of their material needs, prioritizing instead either their relational or subjective wellbeing. A desirable or valued state of wellbeing may also be pursued by means of a concerted effort in two dimensions *(M∩R or M∩S or R∩S)*, but most realistically it will be a combination of all three dimensions together *(M∩R∩S)* – this is where the dimensions of wellbeing intersect. The realization of quality of life can thus be assessed in an integrated and comprehensive manner by looking at this intersection.

Furthermore, a distinction is made between individual and collective wellbeing. Where individual wellbeing concerns those processes and outcomes that determine an individual's quality of life, collective wellbeing refers to the quality of life of a collective (or group) of people. This can be a household, a community or neighborhood, a group of women, men, a social network, or an entire nation's population. It is necessary to distinguish between the two, since human wellbeing stands subject to qualitative transformation when considering how it is aggregated to a higher, collective level. There are often trade-offs between individual and collective wellbeing, and between levels of wellbeing over time. Trade-offs and synergies between individual and collective wellbeing constitute the source of qualitative transformations taking place in the aggregation from the micro to the macro level. People give and take from their individual wellbeing to the greater good or bad, and *vice versa*, and the collective may give back or take from individual wellbeing.

Box 3.5 Emergent process

> The economy is an emergent process, meaning that macroeconomic processes and outcomes emerge through interactions among microeconomic resource agents and resources and through interaction with mesolevel structures and macrolevel aggregates.

Source: McGregor and Pouw (2016)

This adds to an understanding of the complexity of economic decision-making and to an understanding of the economy as an emergent process. Macroeconomic processes and outcomes (e.g. inflation, economic crises) emerge out of microlevel interactions among resource agents, and mesolevel structures. What emerges at the macrolevel may not be entirely predictable from observing microeconomic behavior – there is a certain degree of unexpectedness inherent to complex systems such as the economy. In other words, the properties observed at microeconomic level may not be the same observed as properties of macroeconomic phenomena. For example, macrolevel economic downturn can co-exist with microlevel pockets of sustained income growth.

3.3 The Wellbeing Economics Matrix (WEM)

Together, these five premises provide the building blocks of an inclusive economics framework, which forms the basis for constructing a Wellbeing Economics Matrix (WEM) as presented in Table 3.1. The marked cells represent the focus on the microeconomy of this volume. The WEM resembles a social-accounting matrix (SAM); an economic accounting tool that is used by economic analysts and planners for projecting monetary transactions in an economy, or the outcomes of any changes therein. Statistical bureaus making economic projections make use of SAMs. Similar to a SAM, the WEM also lists resource agents twice, in columns and rows, and provides a roadmap for analyzing resource flows between them. These flows can go into two directions (double-entry): resource agents can be providers (in columns) and recipients (rows) of resource flows at the same time.

It should be noted that there exists five important differences between a WEM and a traditional SAM. The first difference is that the WEM includes 'individuals' apart from 'households' as resource agents in the economy. Second, the WEM also includes 'social groups/communities' as resource agents. Third, Instead of including monetary resource flows in the economy only, the WEM also assesses non-monetary flows

Table 3.1 The Wellbeing Economics Matrix (WEM)

from: Allocation of resources to:	Individuals (I)	Households (H)	Firms (F)	Communities/Social Groups (C)	Government (G)	Rest of the World (W)	Nett Savings (SVf)	Total Received
Individuals (I)	Allocation between Individuals	$Hi= Fi\{Mh\cap Rh\cap Sh\}$	$Fi= Fi\{Mf\cap Rf\cap Sf\}$	$Ci= Fi\{Mc\cap Rc\cap Sc\}$	$Gi= Fi\{Mg\cap Rg\cap Sg\}$	$Wi= Fi\{Mw\cap Rw\cap Sw\}$	SVi	$UiUj\{Hi;Fi;Ci;Gi;Wi;SVi\}$
Households (H)	$Ih= Fh\{Mi\cap Ri\cap Si\}$	Allocation between households	$Fh= Fh\{Mf\cap Rf\cap Sf\}$	$Ch= Fh\{Mc\cap Rc\cap Sc\}$	$Gh= Fh\{Mg\cap Rg\cap Sg\}$	$Wh= Fh\{Mw\cap Rw\cap Sw\}$	SVh	$UhUj\{Ih;Fh;Ch;Gh;Wh;SVh\}$
Firms (F)	$If= Ff\{Mi\cap Ri\cap Si\}$	$Hf= Ff\{Mh\cap Rh\cap Sh\}$	Allocation between firms	$Cf= Ff\{Mc\cap Rc\cap Sc\}$	$Gf= Ff\{Mg\cap Rg\cap Sg\}$	$Wf= Ff\{Mw\cap Rw\cap Sw\}$	SVf	$UfUj\{If;Hf;Cf;Gf;Wf;SVf\}$
Communities (C)	$Ic= Fc\{Mi\cap Ri\cap Si\}$	$Hc= Fc\{Mh\cap Rh\cap Sh\}$	$Fc= Fc\{Mf\cap Rf\cap Sf\}$	Allocation between communities/social groups	$Gc= Fc\{Mg\cap Rg\cap Sg\}$	$Wc= Fc\{Mw\cap Rw\cap Sw\}$	SVc	$UcUj\{Ic;Hc;Fc;Gc;Wc;SVc\}$
Government (G)	$Ig= Fg\{Mi\cap Ri\cap Si\}$	$Hg\ Fg\{Mh\cap Rh\cap Sh\}$	$Fg= Fg\{Mf\cap Rf\cap Sf\}$	$Cg= Fg\{Mc\cap Rc\cap Sc\}$	Allocation between units of government	$Wg= Fg\{Mw\cap Rw\cap Sw\}$	SVg	$UgUj\{Ig;Hg;Fg;Cg;Wg;SVg\}$
Rest of the World (W)	$Iw= Fw\{Mi\cap Ri\cap Si\}$	$Hw= Fw\{Mh\cap Rh\cap$	$Fw= Fw\{Mf\cap Rf\cap Sf\}$	$Cw= Fw\{Mc\cap Rc\cap Sc\}$	$Gw= Fw\{Mg\cap Rg\cap Sg\}$	Allocation between economies	SVw	$UwUj\{Iw;Hw;Fw;Cw;Gw;SVw\}$
Nett Investments (N)	Ni	Nh	Nf	Nc	Ng	Nw	Allocation of investment	$SVi\cap SVh\cap SVf\cap SVc\cap SVg\cap SVw=Ni\cap Nh\cap Nf\cap Nc\cap Ng\cap Nw$
Total Provided	$UjUi\{Ih;If;Ic;Ig;Iw;Ni\}$	$UjUh\{Hi;Hf;Hc;Hg;Hw;Nh\}$	$UjUf\{Fi;Fh;Fc;Fg;Nf\}$	$UjUc\{Ci;Ch;Cf;Cg;Nc\}$	$UjUg\{Gi;Gh;Gf;Gc;Gw;Ng\}$	$UjUw\{Wi;Wh;Wf;Wc;Wg;Nw\}$		Collective Wellbeing

of resources, such as unpaid household goods and services, or gifts and common pool resources. Fourth, the WEM aggregates (but does not simply summate) to collective wellbeing. Fifth, and finally, the WEM is used differently as the SAM; where the diagonal of a SAM is normally left empty, the WEM fills in the diagonal in order to make intra-resource agent trade-offs in wellbeing visible and analyzable. By filling in the diagonal the WEM gives, *prime face*, reason to address inequality in resource allocation, and thus provides a useful entry point for analyzing underling politics of power and social-cultural values. All together, the WEM provides a much broader framework to explore multi-dimensional and multi-level manifestations of wellbeing or illbeing, including gender inequality in the paid and unpaid domains of the economy.

The WEM differentiates 'individuals' *(I)* from 'households' *(H)* (discussed in Chapter 4), and recognizes 'social groups/communities' *(C)* as resource agents (Chapter 5), aside from 'firms' *(F)* (Chapter 5), 'government' *(G)* and the 'rest of the world' *(W)*(both discussed in Volume II – Macroeconomy). 'Nett savings' *(S)* and 'Nett investments' *(N)* close the scheme. Nett savings and investments link the WEM to past and future achievements and evaluations of wellbeing. The WEM is read from column (provider) to row (recipient). The resource flows between resource agents may protect, sustain or enhance wellbeing in one, two or all three dimensions: material wellbeing *(M)*, relational wellbeing *(R)* and subjective wellbeing *(S)*. In order to understand the working of the scheme, let us take an example. We start at column 1, row 2, to consider what resources the individual provides to the household. The individual *(I)* provides to the household (subscript *h*, so therefore *Ih*), material wellbeing *(Mi)*, in the form of income or assets, relational wellbeing *(Ri)*, in the form of social capital and networks, and subjective wellbeing *(Si)*, in the form of satisfaction or quality of life. The nature and sign of this multi-dimensional relationship between the individual and household is specified by the function *Fh*, and is a sub-matrix consisting of three different inter-connected relationships. The amount of material wellbeing provided by the individual to the household is *Mi*≥ 0. The level of relational wellbeing provided by the individual to the household is measured on a different scale, and can only be assessed in quantitative (e.g. time, frequencies) and qualitative terms. The level of subjective wellbeing, whatever indicator is chosen, can only be assessed in qualitative terms (but a Likert scale can be used as one approach to measurement). *Vice versa*, if we mirror *Ih* in the diagonal of the matrix, we can consider what individuals obtain from the household in which they reside, *Hi* (column 2, row 1). The household may provide shelter and food that enhance the material wellbeing of the individual *(Mh)*. The household may also provide a sense of identity and family network to its individual members, which contributes to their relational wellbeing *(Rh)*. Finally, a household may provide a sense of security and personal fulfillment *(Sh)*. The function *Fi* is then the sub-matrix consisting of the above three inter-connected relationships.

Let us consider another example to make sure the scheme is well understood. The flow of resources from where the firm is located (column 3, row 4) to between a firm *(Fc)* and a community. The firm provides employment and economic activity to the community, thus contributing to the material wellbeing of the community *(Mf)*. The firm may conduct its economic activities in an environmentally sustainable or extractive manner, which may enhance or diminish the natural environment *(Rf)*. Finally, the firm may provide future economic and development prospects and a sense of identity to the community *(Sf)*. This explains that a community of people can feel lost when a big company leaves the area to relocate to another place or country. Again, the nature and sign of the relationship is specified by a function *Fc*, consisting of a sub-matrix of the above three inter-connected relationships. *Vice versa*, if we mirror *Fc* in the diagonal, we can explore the flow of scarce resources from the community to the firm, *Cf* (column 4, row 3). A community may provide for the physical space and proximity to natural resources for a firm, which adds to the firm's income and profits *(Mc)*. A community may also provide a concentration of workers and social activities that matter for public relations of the firm *(Rc)*. Finally, the community may foster a public opinion in support or against the economic activities and presence of the firm *(Sc)*. Finally, *Cf* is then the sub-matrix consisting of the above three inter-connected relationships.

The different columns and rows together add up to the total level of individual and collective wellbeing in the economy. To ensure the framework's robustness, each column corresponds to a row. The framework can encompass multiple break-downs (e.g. micro and macro) without losing its robustness. Given that both monetary and non-monetary (e.g. count data, time date) enter the relationships within the sub-matrices and total matrix, these values cannot be simply added up on a uni-dimensional scale. Therefore, we use the intersection sign ($\cap$) each time to indicate that it concerns an intersection of different (submatrices of) relationships. The WEM thus provides a robust framework for a more comprehensive analysis of resource flows between resource agents in the paid and unpaid economy, and how these explain individual and collective levels of wellbeing. The matrix provides a fundamental first step in thinking beyond monetary values of resource flows, and beyond market exchange in the paid economy solely. It provides the basis for exploring new relationships between economic categories of people and resources, formulating new research questions and shedding new light on complex economic problems.

3.4 Learning points

The wellbeing economics framework guides gender-aware economics by considering the economy as a dynamic social process and putting human wellbeing at the centre.

- The economy is defined as an instituted process of resource allocation open to influences from outside.
- Human wellbeing distinguishes between material, socio-relational and subjective wellbeing.
- Resource agents strive to protect, sustain and enhance their wellbeing.
- Resource agents make multiple trade-offs between (i) different dimensions/aspects of wellbeing (ii) individual and collective wellbeing, and (iii) past, present and future wellbeing.
- Economic wellbeing refers to people's command over resources and relations, and satisfaction thereof.
- Economic structure refers to the way in which the economy is organized around its various resource agents, institutions and sectors at multiple levels. The micro, meso, macro and international represent different levels of aggregation in the economy.
- The economy is characterized by emergent properties.

3.5 Assignments and discussion points

Assignment 1 – Determinants of human wellbeing (15 minutes)
Ask students to make a list of things that contribute to their wellbeing in life – it can be anything. After 5 minutes ask them to underline those things that contribute to their material wellbeing – how many items are on the list? Then ask them to count those things that contribute to their relational wellbeing. Which ones are most important to them? (List the top 5). Are they satisfied/content about what they are able to achieve with regard to the listed items? What would they like to improve?

Assignment 2 – Resource agents (15 minutes)
Ask students to team up with their neighbor and draw a picture of themselves as 'resource agents' in the economy. What kind of resources do they make use of on a daily basis? Categorize these in sub-groups. Where do they obtain these resources from (e.g. buy them in the market, obtain

them as free goods and services, public goods and services)? Which resources do they value highly and why? Can they make a ranking of relative priorities over resources?

Discussion point 1 – The economy as an instituted process (20 minutes)
Collect arguments from the group about why the economy is seen as an instituted process of resource allocation, rather than a closed, self-regulating system? (List at least 5 of them). What are the implications of seeing the economy as an instituted process, rather than a system for: (i) people in the economy (ii) economic analysts and (iii) economic policymakers?

Discussion point 2 – Complex economic decisions (20 minutes)
Alex wants to buy himself a new bike. His old bike was stolen. He needs a bike to commute to school every day and to his weekend job in a local cafe. Public transport is too expensive and costs more time. Alex has a limited budget; he can afford to spend 100 Euro right away and buy a bike at the second-hand bicycle shop today. However, he would like to buy a new bike that costs twice as much. Discuss with an immediate neighbor how you think Alex will make his decision. What trade-offs does he make in the process of making this decision? Is the decision all about money?

Discussion point 3 – Security or Green City? (20–25 minutes)
Divide the group of students in two: one group represents a citizens' group of people from a particular insecure city neighborhood X, the other group represent officials from the Town Council whom have to allocate a limited budget to either improving street security at night in neighborhood X or invest in an extension of the City Park to become bigger. The officials from the Town Council are slightly in favour of a greener city because it gives them a good national and international reputation. Each group prepares arguments for and against to be presented at a Town Council meeting in three rounds of 5 minutes: Round (1) presentation of Citizens' group, response of Town Council; Round (2) retreat and discuss in groups. Round (3) presentation of counter-arguments Citizens' group, followed by final decision of Town Council.

Notes

1　System-based thinking in economics is characterized by ascribing one or more of the following features to the economic system: uniformity, fixity in time and place, neutrality and closedness.

2   Other categorizations include the formal versus informal economy, agricultural, industrial and service economy, and the legal versus illegal economy, to serve an analytical purpose.
3   How to start thinking differently about economic performance will be topic of discussion in Chapter 6 Economic Performance.

References and suggested further reading

Bowles, S. and Gintis H. (2013). *A Cooperative Species: Human Reciprocity and Its Evolution*. Princeton: Princeton University Press.

Coyle, D. (2011). *The Economics of Enough. How to Run the Economy as if the Future Matters*. Princeton, NJ: Princeton University Press.

Davis, J.B. (2003). *The Theory of the Individual in Economics: Identity and Value*. New York, NY: Routledge.

Esping-Andersen, G. (1990). *The Three Worlds of Welfare Capitalism*. Cambridge, England: Polity Press.

Fine, B. (2010). *Women's Employment and the Capitalist Family*. New York, NY: Routledge.

Folbre, N. (1993). *Who Pays for the Kids? Gender and the Structure of Constraints*. London, England: Routledge.

Foucault, M. (1978). *The History of Sexuality*. New York, NY: Random House.

Foucault, M. (1982). The subject and power. *Critical Theory*, 8(4), 777–795.

Fullbrook, E. (2009). *Ontology and Economics: Tony Lawson and his critics*. London, England: Routledge.

Golding, I. (2009). *Navigating Our Global Future*. TED Talk, 23 October 2009, last accessed on 12 March 2013, http://blog.ted.com/2009/10/23/navigating_our/.

Gough, I. and McGregor J.A. (2007). *Wellbeing in Developing Countries. From Theory to Practice*. Cambridge: Cambridge University Press.

Gupta, J., Pouw, N. R., and Ros-Tonen, M. A. (2015). Towards an elaborated theory of inclusive development. *The European Journal of Development Research*, 27 (4), 541–559.

Kuiper, E. (2001). *The Most Valuable of all Capital. A Gender Reading of Economic Texts*. Amsterdam, the Netherlands: Thela Thesis.

Lawson, T. (1997). *Economics and Reality*. London, England: Routledge.

Lawson, T. (2003). *Reorienting Economics*. London, England: Routledge.

Lawson, T. (2015). Essays on: The Nature and State of Modern Economics. London, England: Routledge.

Lee, F. (2010). *A History of Heterodox Economics. Challenging the Mainstream in the 20th Century*. London, England: Routledge.

Lutz, M. (1999). *Economics for the Common Good: Two Centuries of Economic Thought in the Humanist Tradition*. London, England: Routledge.

McGregor, J.A. (2004). Researching wellbeing: communicating between the needs of policy makers and the needs of people. *Global Social Policy*, 4(3): 337–358.

McGregor, J.A. (2007) Researching human wellbeing: from concepts to methodology, in Gough I. and McGregor J.A. (eds), *Wellbeing in Developing Countries: From Theory to Research*, Cambridge: Cambridge University Press.

McGregor, J.A. and Pouw N.R.M. (2016) Towards an Economics of Wellbeing, *Cambridge Journal of Economics*, 24 October 2016. https://doi.org/10.1093/cje/bew044

North, D. C. (1990). Institutions and a transaction-cost theory of exchange. Perspectives on positive political economy, 182, 191.

Polanyi, K. (1944). *The Great Transformation*. Boston, MA: Beacon Press.

Pouw, N.R.M. (2011). When growth is empty. Towards an inclusive economics. *The Broker*, 25 (June/July 2011), pp. 4–8.

Pouw, N.R.M. and McGregor J.A. (2014) An Economics of Wellbeing. What would economics look like if it were focused on Human Wellbeing? in *IDS Working Paper 436*, Sussex, England: Institute of Development Studies.

Pouw, N. R., and De Bruijne, A. (2015). Strategic governance for inclusive development. *The European Journal of Development Research*, 27 (4), 481–487.

Sen, A.K. (1977). Rational fools: a critique of the behavioral foundations of economic theory. *Philosophy and Public Affairs*, 6(4): 317–344.

Sen, A.K. (1993). Positional objectivity. *Philosophy and Public Affairs*, 22(2): 126–145.

Sen, A.K. (1999). *Development as Freedom*. New York, NY: Alfred A. Knopf.

Sen, A.K. (2009). *The Idea of Justice*. London: Harvard University Press and Allen Lane.

Simon, H. (1957). *Models of Man, Social and Rational: Mathematical Essays on Rational Human Behavior in a Social Setting*. New York, NY: Wiley.

Staveren, I. van (2001). *The Values of Economics. An Aristotelian Perspective*. New York, NY: Routledge.

Stiglitz, J., Sen, A.K. and Fitoussi J.P. (2009) *Measuring Economic Performance and Social Progress*. Paris: Report by the Commission on Commission on the Measurement of Economic Performance and Social Progress.

WeD (2007) *ESRC Research Statement on Wellbeing. Wellbeing in Development Research Group, University of Bath*, last accessed on 10 December 2011 http://www.welldev.org.uk/research/aims.htm

Wilkinson, R.G. and Pickett K. (2009). *The Spirit Level: Why More Equal Societies Almost Always Do Better*. London, England: Allen Lane.

4   The household economy

4.1 The position and role of households in the economy

The purpose of this chapter is to explain the position and role of households as resource agents in the economy. Individuals are members of households, in which they may or may not reside (see Figure 4.1). For gender-aware economic analysis individual women and men are distinguished from the household. The household plays an important role in the unpaid economy, alongside social groups and communities of people (discussed in Chapter 5). The household comes in many different types. The household engages in the production of goods and services to provide for its needs, as well as in the consumption and distribution of all kinds of goods and services. The household economy is alternatively referred to as the 'care economy' because of the caring services being provided as a one of its core functions. Because of the multiple roles as producer, consumer and distributor of resources, the household is often referred to as an economy in itself. The household economy is positioned in the unpaid economy, but has multiple inter-connections with the paid economy. Clearly exploring these inter-connections helps to understand how intra-household trade-offs are made, and how economic wellbeing is pursued (or 'illbeing' experienced).

Unpaid household work contributes to household and individual economic wellbeing. An individual's/household economic wellbeing refers to the individual/household command over resources (e.g. assets, time, money, capabilities) and relations with others (e.g. colleagues, friends, neighbors) and the environment (e.g. as consumers and producers, citizens), and people's goals and satisfaction thereof (in terms of subjective evaluations). Individual and household economic wellbeing is depicted in Figure 4.1.

Box 4.1 Individual/household economic wellbeing

> Individual/household economic wellbeing refers to the command over resources, relations, goals and satisfaction thereof.

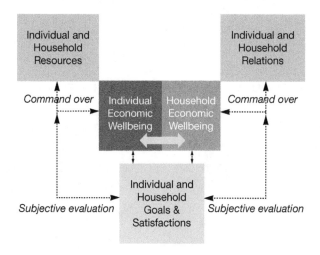

Figure 4.1 Individual and household economic wellbeing.

A substantial amount of people's time and energy goes into unpaid household work. Together with leisure time, unpaid household work enhances human capital, intra- and inter-household relationships, reproduces and regenerates the labor force through providing care, and contributes to subjective economic wellbeing. Unpaid household work can act both as a leverage and constraint to women's and men's available time to work in the paid economy; there is a trade-off between working in the unpaid and paid economy. Economic decisions about the division of unpaid household work are not solely made within the realm of the household; these decisions are influenced and permeated by gender relations and other social and political institutions (see Figure 4.2).

Because of power inequalities within the household, gender inequalities in economic wellbeing can emerge. A gender-aware economic wellbeing model of the household enables us to analyze intra-household differences. In many cultures and societies women spend on average more time on unpaid household work than men do, although this trend is changing. It is important to include unpaid household work in economic analysis and policy formulation. Gender-aware indicators can shed light on women's and men's time burdens, and their respective shares in unpaid household work. These indicators are useful for defining benchmarks and policy objectives, and evaluating impact of social and economic policy-making. From a gender-aware economics approach these policies and measures are geared to strengthen and support the quality and efficiency of the household economy, because it brings benefits to the economy as a whole.

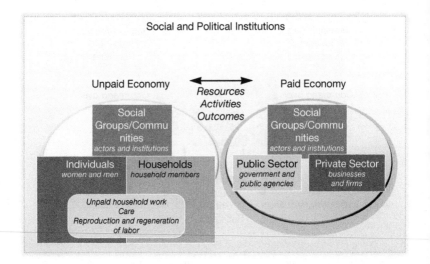

Figure 4.2 The positions and roles of individuals and households in the economy.

4.2 The household defined

The household is broadly defined as a group of individual members whom provide for their wellbeing collectively. The household may consist of a family, but it may also include other, non-related members. Households come in different types: compositions and sizes differ across culture, time and place. It is difficult to select one definition that captures all household types. The household is a resource agent because it solves economic problems by allocating resources. The household is also a social institution, with norms, rules and codes of conduct implicitly and explicitly defined. Some of these rules and codes of conduct may be more formally defined, for example in a marriage contract or cohabitation agreement. Others concern unwritten rules and norms that influence individuals' status and relationships within the household. Intra-household differences in access and command over resources prevail between individual household members, according to gender, age or family status.

Box 4.2 The household

The household is a group of individual members whom provide for their economic wellbeing collectively. The household is both a resource agent and social institution.

Differences in natural, demographic, social/cultural and political/economic circumstances lead to households experiencing very different living conditions. In overcrowded Mumbai, India, it is discomforting to see entire families camping on the sidewalks at night because they have nowhere else to go. The one-child family planning policy in China has resulted in many parents having one child only, with many births having been averted between 1979 and 2009 – an estimated 200 million, with detrimental effects on the female gender because of underreporting female births, abortions and infanticide. Where the extended family is a common phenomenon in rural Africa, families with grandparents co-residing are more familiar in Latin America and Asian countries, and also in Southern Europe and other parts of the world. The nuclear family used to be an exclusive Western phenomenon, but has spread around the world, especially into the large cities. The number of single-person and single-headed households is also increasing rapidly in urban environments. The HIV/Aids pandemic has resulted in a dramatic rise of child-headed households in many sub-Saharan African countries. Different definitions of the household have been used in data collection, surveys and economic analysis. A myriad of household types is presented in Box 4.3.

Box 4.3 A myriad of household types

- **Single-person household** = a single (often) adult woman or man residing in a housing unit.
- **Female-headed household** = a family, nuclear or extended, headed by a *de facto* or *de jure* single woman (a divorcée, widow, non-married or co-wife in polygamous system with the husband/partner residing elsewhere).
- **Male-headed household** = a family, nuclear or extended, headed by a male head of household (husband or other senior male) and commonly with a woman (wife/partner) present.
- **Orphan-headed household** = a family group comprised of children and headed by one child (or more children).
- **Extended family** = a family group comprised of parents, child(ren), and other close relatives (grand-parents, cousins) residing in the same house or compound.
- **Hearth-hold** = co-residential unit of women and their dependents sharing the food and living together with other hearth-holds in a compound.
- **Nuclear family** = a family comprised of husband and wife and their child(ren).
- **Single-parent family** = a family comprised of one parent living together with her/his child(ren).

Sources: Ekejiuba (1995); Cornwall (2005) and national statistical bureaus.

4.3 Inequality and power relations in the household

It should be noted that in any collective of people, such as the household, there is no guarantee of unity among its members. Unity is conducive to cooperation and mutual support; conflict can undermine unity and lead to disruption, abuse and violence. Personality differences and inequalities in gender, age, knowledge, skills and power are some of the reasons why the allocation of resources within households may generate unequal individual economic wellbeing outcomes. Some household members exercise more power than others in deciding who gets what and why. The power to have a voice and exert control within the household is co-determined by social institutions and power relations outside the household and embedded in a social-cultural and political environment. As such, the household itself is a social institution. Intra-household relations between female and male household members are often a reflection of society-wide gender relations. This is why we see women having less voice and control in intra-household decision making in traditional patriarchal and patrilineal societies, than in modern and/or matriarchal and matrilineal societies. This leads to intra-household gender inequalities in human capital investments – nutrition, education and health, but also influences how gender identity, roles and relations are performed. Domination of male household members over female household members, or *vice versa*, can lead to suppression, silencing, abuse and violence. Domestic violence is a sensitive issue, which remains largely hidden because of a culture of silence and shame. Domestic violence, including wife beating, is still thought to be acceptable in many patriarchal societies. In countries where child marriage is practiced, girls marry as early as age 12, despite that this is a human rights violation.

In 2013, the World Bank has drawn worldwide attention to the problem of gender-based violence in their annual world development report. One out of three women have experienced gender-based violence in their life, and many men have been victims as well. Gender-based violence is not only a human rights violation, but also causes major health, social and economic problems affecting productivity and earnings, not allowing people to function well and without fear as members of households (World Bank, 2013).

Box 4.4 Gender-based violence

Gender-based violence (GBV) is the general term used to capture violence that occurs as a result of the normative role expectations associated with each gender, along with the unequal power relationships between the two genders, within the context of a specific society.

Source: Bloom (2008, p. 14).

The Social Institutions and Gender Index (SIGI) developed by the Organisation of Economic Co-operation and Development (OECD) aims to capture violence against women as part of their restricted physical integrity, which is one of five institutional gender discriminations in society that shape intra-household relations and women's social identity as compared with men's. The SIGI consists of five indices constructed out of 14 variables capturing social attitudes, laws, health outcome indicators and quotas, including: (i) Discriminatory family code; (ii) Restricted civil liberties; (iii) Restricted physical integrity; (iv) Son bias; and (v) Restricted resources and entitlements (see Figure 4.3).

Each indicator is subjectively assessed on a numerical scale from 1 to 5 and weighs equally in the composite index. In 2012 the OECD had collected data for 86 developing countries[1] in total. The first 20 countries with the highest gender discrimination are listed in Table 4.1. Out of these 20, 16 countries are located in Africa, and four in Western or Central Asia. Argentina was listed as the country with the lowest gender discrimination in 2012, out of the selected 86 countries, followed closely by Costa Rica and Paraguay.

Intra-household gender differences are also reflected in gender tasks and responsibilities. For example, in many households women have a greater responsibility as food providers, whereas men are considered the main household head and income provider. The women's sphere of influence is stretched out over the entire agricultural production system among smallholder farmers in sub-Saharan Africa. Increasingly, in rural economies young men are migrating into cities, leaving women in (partial) command over the land and production activities. In small-scale coastal communities where people fish for an income and personal

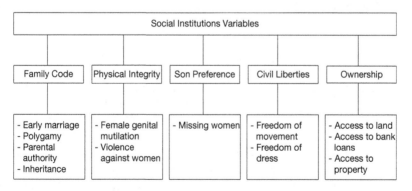

Figure 4.3 Composition of the social institutions and gender index (SIGI).
Source: OECD (2014).

Table 4.1 Twenty countries where SIGI scores highest, 2012

Country	SIGI score*
1. Mali	0.600977
2. Sudan	0.525095
3. Congo, Democratic Republic	0.513559
4. Yemen	0.506513
5. Somalia	0.499246
6. Benin	0.456945
7. Chad	0.452535
8. Nigeria	0.442831
9. Guinea	0.439627
10. Gabon	0.428793
11. Gambia, The	0.393300
12. Syrian Arab Republic	0.392839
13. Swaziland	0.391463
14. Uganda	0.383802
15. Niger	0.372019
16. Cameroon	0.369592
17. Burkina Faso	0.368684
18. Afghanistan	0.363417
19. Azerbaijan	0.362053
20. Togo	0.360838

*The SIGI score ranges from 0 (lowest) to 1 (highest discrimination).
Source: OECD (2014).

consumption, men dominate the fishing activities of the family, whereas women dominate the processing side. Although, there exist also fishing communities where women are allowed to fish themselves. In family businesses, women's labor is often considered 'free labor' and subject to control by men. However, traditional gender patterns are shifting and so do women's and men's roles in the household economy. Gender performances differ between women and men, but exceptions and change co-emerge and caution is needed to prevent stereotyping and simplistic generalizations.

4.4 The household economy: activities, resources and outcomes

Households and individuals, together with social groups and communities (see Chapter 5) constitute the unpaid economy. Individuals are analytically separated from households, since this enables intra-household gender analysis. However, when speaking of 'households' individuals are also implied. Households engage in unpaid household work and the reproduction and regeneration of labor as their core activities (see Figure 4.4). The household also provides care to its members. Childcare in families is a prime form of intra-household care. But care of oneself and other household members, elderly and sick, are also important caring services.

Resources used for unpaid household work are obtained from different sources. Households use their available time, space and resources to produce food and other commodities. Goods and services are bought in

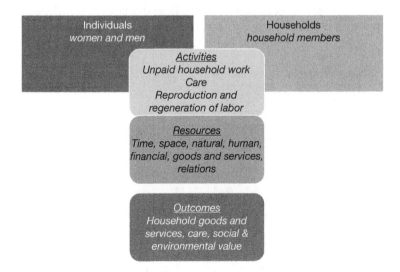

Figure 4.4 The household economy: activities, resources and outcomes.

the market, or obtained as free gifts or through exchange in-kind. For example, ceremonial gifts for a wedding or funeral. Finally, pubic goods and services may be obtained from the government or a public agency, as subsidized or non-subsidized goods and services (e.g. free primary education). Households furthermore engage in social relationships to arrange access to resources, participate in joint activities, and share in outcomes (e.g. sharing a festive meal), or provide for these (e.g. providing family care to kins). Last but not least, caring services are delivered by the household to its individual members, merely by investing time and attention, which has intrinsic value.

The activities undertaken in the household economy contribute to household economic wellbeing (WB_H) and individual economic wellbeing (WB_I) in a material and social-relational sense, and also subjectively. The wellbeing outcomes achieved may hold immediate value, for example when a household is enjoying a home-cooked meal. Economic wellbeing outcomes can also lie in the future, for example when parents invest in their children's education. Economic wellbeing outcomes, and the process leading towards it, are not gender neutral. In the household economy we distinguish between women's economic wellbeing (WB_f) and men's economic wellbeing (WB_m) (see Figure 4.5). As Amartya Sen explained, the household is a locus of cooperation and conflict, with sometimes significant wellbeing differences, in process and outcomes for women and men, girls and boys. Unequal power relations are at the origin of many gender inequalities in roles, relationships and outcomes (1987).

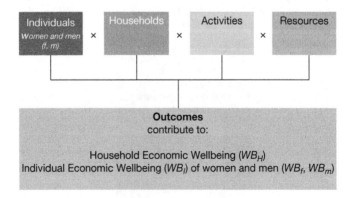

Figure 4.5 Household goods and services contribute to household and individual economic wellbeing.

4.5 Modeling individual economic wellbeing

In this section we zoom in on the relationship between unpaid household work and individual and household economic wellbeing. Individuals are 'nested' within households, or form a household on their own in the case of single person. Let us consider here the example of an individual residing in a household consisting of two or more members. It is assumed that individuals strive to improve, sustain or protect individual economic wellbeing (WB_i), as well as household economic wellbeing (WB_h). Individual economic wellbeing is then the difference between what the individual receives from the household in the form of household material (M_h), relational (R_h) and subjective wellbeing (S_h), and what the individual provides to the household in the form of its individual supply of material (M_i), relational (R_i) and subjective wellbeing (S_i).

In the original Wellbeing Economics Matrix (WEM) in Table 1 (Chapter 3) this corresponds to the first row entry, minus the first column entry, being equal to:

$$WB_i = U_i U_j \{H_i\} - U_j U_i \{I_h\} \tag{4.1}$$

or, written in full functional form:

$$WB_i = F_i \{M_h \cap R_h \cap C_h\} - F_h \{M_i \cap R_i \cap C_i\} \tag{4.2}$$

Because of gendered identities, roles and power differences in the household, women and men may achieve different levels of economic wellbeing within the household (or independent thereof). This is why it is useful to analyze individual economic wellbeing differently from household-level economic wellbeing. There may be certain advantages of forming a household with others as opposed to an individual; there may also be disadvantages in any one, two or three dimensions of wellbeing.

Building on (Eq 4.2), the subscript i can be replaced by f or m to derive the individual economic wellbeing functions of the female and male members of the household respectively, as follows:

$$WB_f = F_f \{M_h \cap R_h \cap C_h\} - F_h \{M_f \cap R_f \cap C_f\} \tag{4.3}$$

$$WB_m = F_m \{M_h \cap R_h \cap C_h\} - F_h \{M_m \cap R_m \cap C_m\} \tag{4.4}$$

The three economic wellbeing dimensions can be concretized by means of specifying the variables used in the analysis.[2] For example, in material sense, female and male members provide a certain amount of individual income $(I_{f,m})$ and assets $(A_{f,m})$ to the household. This leads to the formulation of the following sub-matrix (Eq 4.5) of household material wellbeing:

$$\text{Individual material wellbeing} = \begin{bmatrix} M_f = \left\{ \begin{array}{c} I_f \\ A_f \end{array} \right\} \\ M_m = \left\{ \begin{array}{c} I_m \\ A_m \end{array} \right\} \end{bmatrix} \tag{4.5}$$

In relational sense each member brings in a set of qualities into the household; for example, her/his connections to other social groups $(SG_{f,m})$ and political connections $(PC_{f,m})$. These form input into the following sub-matrix (Eq 4.6) of individual relational wellbeing:

$$\text{Individual relational wellbeing} = \begin{bmatrix} R_f = \left\{ \begin{array}{c} SG_f \\ PC_f \end{array} \right\} \\ R_m = \left\{ \begin{array}{c} SG_m \\ PC_m \end{array} \right\} \end{bmatrix} \tag{4.6}$$

Both can be assessed in quantitative terms (number of groups/connections) or in qualitative sense (quality of relationship). In the latter case, a Likert scale technique can be adopted to assess the subjective evaluation of the quality of a relationship on an ordinal scale.

Finally, female and male household members will evaluate what they can achieve in a material and relational sense by expressing their satisfactions or dissatisfactions. For example, they experience a sense of self-worthiness $(SW_{f,m})$ and happiness $(HA_{f,m})$. These can only be assessed in subjective terms, by means of self-perceptions or inter-personal evaluations. This leads to the formulation of a third sub-matrix of individual subjective wellbeing, consisting of a set of qualitative measures exclusively:

$$\text{Individual subjective wellbeing} = \begin{bmatrix} S_f = \left\{ \begin{array}{c} SW_f \\ HA_f \end{array} \right\} \\ S_m = \left\{ \begin{array}{c} SW_m \\ HA_m \end{array} \right\} \end{bmatrix} \tag{4.7}$$

Together, these sub-matrices combine into what female and male members provide to the household in total. Since the vector variables within each sub-matrix use different underlying scales of measurement, they cannot be simply added-up through summation (+). Instead, we use the intersection term instead (∩), as in the equations below.

$$\textit{Female provisions to the household} = F_h \left\{ \begin{Bmatrix} I_f \\ A_f \end{Bmatrix} \cap \begin{Bmatrix} SG_f \\ PC_f \end{Bmatrix} \cap \begin{Bmatrix} SW_f \\ HA_f \end{Bmatrix} \right\}$$

(4.8)

and

$$\textit{Male provisions to the household} = M_h \left\{ \begin{Bmatrix} I_m \\ A_m \end{Bmatrix} \cap \begin{Bmatrix} SG_m \\ PC_m \end{Bmatrix} \cap \begin{Bmatrix} SW_m \\ HA_m \end{Bmatrix} \right\}$$

(4.9)

Similarly, we can analyze what female and male members receive from the household in terms of material, relational and subjective resources. Using the same vector variables, this implies specifying the following set of equations:

$$\textit{Female receipts from the household} = F_f \left\{ \begin{Bmatrix} I_h \\ A_h \end{Bmatrix} \cap \begin{Bmatrix} SG_h \\ PC_h \end{Bmatrix} \cap \begin{Bmatrix} SW_h \\ HA_h \end{Bmatrix} \right\}$$

(4.10)

and

$$\textit{Male receipts from the household} = F_m \left\{ \begin{Bmatrix} I_h \\ A_h \end{Bmatrix} \cap \begin{Bmatrix} SG_h \\ PC_h \end{Bmatrix} \cap \begin{Bmatrix} SW_h \\ HA_h \end{Bmatrix} \right\}$$

(4.11)

This brings us to the specific assessment of female and male wellbeing achieved as members of households in the following terms:

$$WB_f = F_f \left\{ \begin{Bmatrix} I_h \\ A_h \end{Bmatrix} \cap \begin{Bmatrix} SG_h \\ PC_h \end{Bmatrix} \cap \begin{Bmatrix} SW_h \\ HA_h \end{Bmatrix} \right\}$$
$$- F_h \left\{ \begin{Bmatrix} I_f \\ A_f \end{Bmatrix} \cap \begin{Bmatrix} SG_f \\ PC_f \end{Bmatrix} \cap \begin{Bmatrix} SW_f \\ HA_f \end{Bmatrix} \right\}$$

(4.12)

And

$$WB_m = F_m \left\{ \left\{ \begin{matrix} I_h \\ A_h \end{matrix} \right\} \cap \left\{ \begin{matrix} SG_h \\ PC_h \end{matrix} \right\} \cap \left\{ \begin{matrix} SW_h \\ HA_h \end{matrix} \right\} \right\}$$

$$- M_h \left\{ \left\{ \begin{matrix} I_m \\ A_m \end{matrix} \right\} \cap \left\{ \begin{matrix} SG_m \\ PC_m \end{matrix} \right\} \cap \left\{ \begin{matrix} SW_m \\ HA_m \end{matrix} \right\} \right\} \tag{4.13}$$

Women and men, girls and boys may thus achieve different levels of economic wellbeing *(WB_f, WB_m)* due to gender differences. This can be expressed as their individual wellbeing carries a different weight *(π)* in total household wellbeing. Intra-household individual differences in wellbeing are inter-dependent, but together they constitute household wellbeing, which is then formulated as follows:

$$WB_h = \pi \cdot WB_f \cap (1-\pi) \cdot WB_m \tag{4.14}$$

4.6 Modeling household economic wellbeing

Consider next the example of a household striving to improve, sustain or protect household economic wellbeing *(WB_h)*. Household economic wellbeing is then the difference between what the household receives from individuals *(I_h)*, other households *(H_h)*, firms *(F_h)*, communities/social groups *(C_h)*, and government *(G_h)*, and what their net savings *(SV_h)* are in the form of goods and services contributing to material *(M_i; M_h; M_f; M_g)*, relational *(R_i; R_h; R_f; R_g)*, and subjective economic wellbeing *(S_i; S_h; S_f; S_g)* minus what the household provides or delivers to individuals *(H_i)*, other households *(H_h)*, firms *(H_f)*, communities/social groups *(H_c)*, and government *H_g)*, and what their net investments are *(N_h)*, in terms of material *(M_c)*, relational *(R_c)* and subjective economic wellbeing *(S_c)*.

In the original WEM in Table 1 (Chapter 3) this corresponds to the second column entries from the left, minus the second row entries from the top, being equal to:

$$WB_h = U_h U_j \{I_h; H_h; F_h; C_h; G_h; SV_h\} - U_j U_h \{H_i; H_h; H_f; H_c; H_g; N_h\} \tag{4.15}$$

or, written in full functional form:

$$WB_h = U_h U_j \{ F_h \{ M_i \cap R_i \cap S_i \}; \; F_h \{ M_h \cap R_h \cap S_h \};$$
$$F_h \{ M_f \cap R_f \cap S_f \}; F_h \{ M_c \cap R_c \cap S_c \}; F_h \{ M_g \cap R_g \cap S_g \};$$
$$SV_h \} - U_j U_h \{ F_i \{ M_h \cap R_h \cap S_h \}; F_h \{ M_h \cap R_h \cap S_h \};$$
$$F_f \{ M_h \cap R_h \cap S_h \}; F_c \{ M_h \cap R_h \cap S_h \}; F_g \{ M_h \cap R_h \cap S_h \}; N_h \}$$

$$(4.16)$$

The concretization subsequently takes place in the same way as in the example of individual economic wellbeing above. This leaves us to investigate inter-household differences in economic wellbeing by comparing the wellbeing of one household WB_{h1} to that of another household WB_{h2} in the multiple dimensions of wellbeing.

The above series of equations have made the different sources of individual and household economic wellbeing more transparent by operating the three wellbeing dimensions into concrete concepts and variables that can be measured. They remain, however, theoretical relationships. Only after testing the relationships based on empirical data, can their functional forms be specified.

4.7 Advantages of scale in households

By living together a household can benefit physically, socially and mentally from sharing resources, activities and generated outcomes. In such a way, more efficient use can be made of valuable assets and goods, such as a house or a car. At the same time, unpaid household work can be performed more efficiently when sharing tasks and responsibilities, such as the caring of children. Finally, the act of sharing between household members in itself may hold intrinsic value to the persons involved. These advantages create positive returns to scale that can be measured, either in quantitative or on qualitative sense.

Returns to scale refer to the efficiency of the relationship between inputs (labor and resources) and outputs produced (household goods and services). Returns to scale can be increasing, constant/neutral or decreasing:

I   increasing returns to scale: if output increases by more than the proportional change in inputs;
II constant returns to scale: if output increases by the same proportional change in inputs; and
III decreasing returns to scale; if output increases by less than the proportional change in input.

An example of increasing returns to scale would be if two individual household members can organize their agricultural production work more efficiently by collaboration instead of working in separate fields. They can allocate their time more efficiently, for example, because they have supplementary skills and tools. The efficiency gain translates in an increase in average output per person and can be measured. In this example, output may be measured in terms of acres of land worked per person per hour. The efficiency gain is the difference between the acres of land worked p/ person p/hour in the case of collaboration and non-collaboration. This can also be written in an economic formula, as follows: $\Delta \dfrac{Acres\ per\ person}{hour}$, whereby the sigma sign (Δ) indicates the difference in output between collaboration and non-collaboration. If this difference is positive, there will be an increasing return to scale. However, if in the above example there is no efficiency gain from collaboration in terms of increased output per person, then the difference will be equal to zero and we speak of constant returns to scale. Finally, if the collaboration, for one reason or the other, creates inefficiencies that lower output p/person p/hour, the difference will be negative, which is a case of decreasing returns to scale. The latter could happen, for example, in the case of the field being too small relative to the number of people working in it, thus getting in each other's way.

The above is an example whereby household members can potentially realize a benefit in the material sense through joining forces. We can think of similar gains of sharing other household production activities between two or more members of households. The efficiency gain translates into a material increase in output, which contributes to the material wellbeing of the household. Apart from contributions (or reductions) to material wellbeing, the formation of a household itself and intra-household collaboration in production, consumption and distribution activities can also affect the quality of intra-household relationships. In that case, there are potential advantages of scale to the household's social/relational wellbeing. These returns cannot be measured in the same way as material wellbeing. For example, in the positive sense, intra-household collaboration can strengthen family ties and increase inter-personal trust. Collaboration can also increase the likelihood of working jointly in other household activities and tasks, and stimulate reciprocity and altruism in the household. The social/relational return to intra-household collaboration is difficult to measure in quantitative terms because it involves qualitative (subjective) judgments. By using Likert scales[3], personal judgments and opinions or feelings can be translated into an ordinal scale thus making indicator construction possible. For example, inter-personal trust (T) can be measured on a scale from 1 to 5, whereby 1=no trust, 2=low trust, 3=average trust, 4=high trust and 5=very high trust. In a household of size (n) household trust (HT) can then be measured by summing up (Σ) the levels of trust T_i that individual household members (i) have in other household members (j), whereby $(i \neq j)$, so that $HT = \Sigma(T_{i,j}) / n$. Measuring the difference in household trust between the case of collaboration and non-collaboration simply involves measuring ΔHT. If this difference is positive, it means that household trust has increased in members collaborating. If the difference is zero, there are no perceived gains in household trust, or, individual differences balance out to zero. If the difference is negative, household trust has been diminished from the act of collaboration.

Finally, individuals may also intrinsically value being members of a household and derive joy and contentment from intra-household collaboration. In that case, there exists potential advantages of scale to their subjective economic wellbeing. Again, this would involve a subjective assessment that is difficult to quantify. By using the Likert scale we can measure the subjective returns. For example, if we are interested in the level of household contentment (HC), this can be measured by summing up (Σ) the levels of contentment S_i that individual household members (i) experience, so that $HC = \Sigma(S_i) / n$. Measuring the difference in subjective economic wellbeing between collaboration and non-collaboration then involves measuring ΔHC.

Box 4.5 Returns to scale

Returns to scale refer to the efficiency of the relationship between inputs (labor and resources) and outputs produced (goods and services). Returns to scale can be increasing, constant/neutral or decreasing.

4.8 The value of unpaid household work

Unpaid household work contributes to the economic wellbeing of the household and its individual members. Unpaid household work is a type of public good that has positive externalities to other domains of the economy. Without unpaid household work, people will fail to fulfill (parts of) their material, social/relational and psychological needs. In the household economy, material and immaterial goods and services are produced, including food, shelter, hygiene and sanitation, education, and care. In addition to this, the household intrinsically provides a family environment and a place to call home. The care, feeding, shelter and education services provided at home improve the quality of the labor force, but also contribute positively to cohesion, peace and stability in the unpaid economy.

Household members engage in unpaid household work on the basis of relationships of reciprocity and mutual support. Reciprocity is the expectation that people will return a gift or act of kindness in a similar way. Reciprocity can also be negative, meaning that people will respond to hurt or harm with indifference or retaliation. Reciprocity can be direct – expecting a personal return in the immediate future – or more subtle, as in the case of delayed reciprocity or voluntary forms of mutual support. Relationships of reciprocity and mutual support, by and large, structure the allocation of scarce resources within the household economy, and between individual household members. People assign value to such relationships because of love, moral obligation, a sense of fairness and justice, customary practice, habit and belief.

Women and men spend time and energy on unpaid household work. The time spent on unpaid household work cannot be spent on paid labor because everyone's time is finite; the two activities are mutually exclusive, unless multi-tasking is an option (e.g. babysitting whilst computer programming at home). There are only 24 hours in a day, and people need time for leisure and rest. To overburden people would deteriorate the quality of unpaid household work, but also impact on the quality of the labor force and the larger economy. In economics, we say there is an opportunity cost to unpaid household work. The opportunity cost of unpaid household work in a narrow, monetary sense refers to the income foregone by not spending time on paid work. The opportunity cost of unpaid household work can therefore be measured. We will look into the issue of measurement of unpaid household work in Section 4.5. In a broad, non-monetary sense, opportunity costs can also entail foregone career opportunities and job satisfaction by not spending time on paid work. This is more difficult to measure since it involves a series of hypothetical events.

There is also an opportunity cost to paid work. The amount of time spent on paid work cannot be spent on unpaid household work; for example on childcare or spending time with family members and deriving a certain level of satisfaction from that. Economic agents need to trade off paid and unpaid household work in a way that balances their needs and ambitions, opportunities and constraints in a satisfactory manner. However, the opportunity cost of unpaid household work is never measured in national statistics; yet, it enters the equation when people make decisions on how to best allocate their scarce time to paid and unpaid work. In making this trade off, economic agents use 'time' as principle measure and weigh this against a set of personal/shared values ascribed to each activity.

Box 4.6 The opportunity cost of time

> The monetary and non-monetary cost of the forgone economic activity
> after making a choice between spending time on one economic activity or
> the other.

The opportunity costs of both unpaid and paid work thus play an important role in the daily economic decisions of women and men. We have pointed out that there are quantitative (monetary, or time) aspects to these opportunity costs, as well as qualitative aspects (attention, care). Because of gendered identities, roles and relationships, women and men may weigh these opportunity costs differently. The opportunity cost of paid work may be higher to women if society expects her to fulfill all childcare tasks at home. Sometimes, for women *not* to spend time at home is not an option because of cultural norms and traditions. Although, household income is always needed, these women are largely dependent upon the income earned by a male household member. In that case, gender norms act as a constraint on women's time spent in the paid labor market. In many societies these days, men are also expected to perform a fair amount of unpaid household work. This influences their decisions about paid work as well. Women spend on average more time on unpaid household work than men. For example, in the US between 2003–2007, women performed an average of 10.8 hours more per week on unpaid household work than men (see Figure 4.6). A 1995 UN report, measuring the amount of unpaid household work in

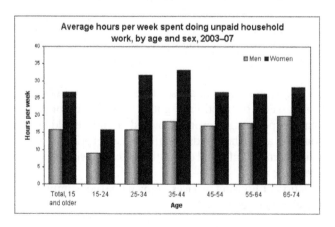

Figure 4.6 Distribution of unpaid household work between women and men in the U.S., 2003–2007.

14 countries, estimated that globally as much time is invested in unpaid household work as in paid work. The value of unpaid household work is estimated to constitute 35–55% of the total GDP. Globally, the balance is shifting slowly toward a more equal distribution of unpaid household work between women and men due to women's increasing participation in the paid labor market and a broader cultural acceptance of men performing unpaid household work. However, women's relative share in leisure time is still significantly smaller than men's.

4.9 The measurement of unpaid household work

Thus far we have explained that unpaid household work contributes to household and individual economic wellbeing and has an opportunity cost because of the investment of time. Unpaid household work brings many positive externalities to the economy as a whole. Yet, the value of unpaid household work is not reflected in the dominant measure of economic performance, GDP. We will discuss economic performance and GDP growth in Chapter 7. In this section we concentrate on the measurement of unpaid household work.[4]

Unpaid household work is not systematically counted as part of total economic output, measured by gross domestic product (GDP). In 1993, the UN System of National Accounts (SNA) created an opportunity to integrate unpaid household work in national accounting frameworks. Through the concept of 'Satellite Accounts', the SNA accommodated the use of additional dimensions to 'National Accounts' by means of new concepts and measures that capture (aspects of) unpaid household work. According to the SNA, unpaid household work that can be incorporated in complementary satellite accounts includes:

I   unpaid services for own final use (domestic and care-giving services);
II   informal sector production of goods and services for own final use by unincorporated enterprises owned by households (subsistence production and other kinds of informal enterprises);
III unpaid volunteer/informal domestic and care-giving services to other households; and
IV   production of housing services for own final consumption (imputed rents of owner-occupied housing).

The conceptual distinction between production and consumption activities (leisure), in a household is not so clear-cut. Cooking a meal at home and subsequently eating it involves a production and consumption activity combined. Playing a football game with your kids is considered leisure – not the production of a childcare service. The third-person criterion is used to differentiate production from consumption by stating that if a person can buy a market replacement be bought (for example, dinner in a restaurant), or someone can be paid to do the activity on the person's behalf (a home-cook), it is considered a production activity. In theory, there is a market substitute available that could replace the person's unpaid household production at a certain price. This does not resolve the problem entirely, but is one step in the direction of clarity of conceptualization.

Box 4.7 The third person criterion

> The third person criterion says that an activity should be considered to be production (rather than leisure) if a person could buy a market replacement or pay someone to do the activity in his or her place. The criterion is used to distinguish between unpaid household production and consumption activities.

Source: Goodwin et al. (2008).

Time use measures are useful to count women's and men's contributions to unpaid work. Time use measures are also useful to compute the total time burden of unpaid and paid work together on women and men. As explained before, time cannot be assumed to be infinitely available. By assigning a wage value to unpaid household work, we can compare its value more easily to income from paid labor and aggregate it to compare with total GDP in an economy. Four methods exist to assign a market wage value to unpaid household work:

1 the mean wage approach – using the mean wage in the economy as a whole and assigning this wage to each hour of unpaid household work. Separate means are usually calculated for women's and men's wage in the economy, as women's wages on average tend to be lower than men's.
2 the opportunity cost approach – estimating the wage that the person would have earned if she/he had not done the unpaid household work.
3 the generalist approach – using the mean wage of workers who perform similar work to the unpaid household work, but who are

employed in a paid job (for example, the wage of domestic workers and the wage of childcare workers).

4　the specialist approach – focusing on the activity rather than on the person performing the activity. For each activity it uses the wage earned by paid workers, whose functions and circumstances are comparable to the unpaid work concerned (for example, cooking could be valued at the wage of a paid chef or cook, while time spent on house maintenance could be valued at the wage of a paid carpenter).

There are two complexities involved in the above procedures. The first complexity is the occurrence of multi-tasking – that is, performing multiple unpaid household work or paid and unpaid work at the same time. This is usually resolved by counting the most dominant activity only. The second complexity is to find the most appropriate market wages for different household work activities involving different skill levels (option 1), and in situations where a valid or realistic market equivalent is not present – for example, in a rural, non-monetized economy where permanent wage work is rare and instead most labor is subsistence labor (option 2). If these complexities cannot be overcome it is advisable to use time use measures only. What approach is used to assign a monetary value to unpaid household work (mean wage; opportunity cost; generalist; specialist) is a decision made by the statistical bureau and can differ across countries. The monetary valuation is important to compare unpaid household production as a fictitious monetary flow in the Satellite Accounts, with the value of paid production in the National Accounts. We will simply refer to this monetary value of unpaid work, independent of method, as the market wage value.[5] For now we concentrate on the micro economic valuation of unpaid household work and the formulation of gender indicators at this level.

To shed light on the gender division of unpaid household work, and respective shares in total household income, the following set of indicators can be used:

- ***Women's and men's time shares in unpaid household work:***

$$\textit{Women's time share in unpaid household work} = \frac{TUW_f}{TUW_H} \cdot 100\%$$

$$\textit{Men's time share in unpaid household work} = \frac{TUW_m}{TUW_H} \cdot 100\%$$

$$\text{Gender division of time spent on unpaid household work} = \frac{TUW_f}{TUW_m} \cdot 100\%$$

Whereby, TUW_H stands for total household time spent on unpaid household work.

- **The value of unpaid household work and women's and men's contributions:**

  Value of unpaid household work provided by women $= TUW_f \cdot MW_f$

  Value of unpaid household work provided by men $= TUW_m \cdot MW_m$

  Gender division of total value of unpaid household work
  $$= \frac{TUW_f \cdot MW_f}{TUW_m \cdot MW_m} \cdot 100\%$$

Whereby, MW_i stands for the market wage value of unpaid household work of individual i.

- **Women's and men's shares of unpaid household work in total household income:**

  Women's share of unpaid household work in household income
  $$= \frac{TUW_f \cdot MW_f}{HHI} \cdot 100\%$$

  Men's share in market wage value of unpaid household work
  $$= \frac{TUW_m \cdot MW_m}{HHI} \cdot 100\%$$

  Gender division of market wage value of unpaid household work
  $$= \frac{TUW_f \cdot MW_f}{TUW_m \cdot MW_m} \cdot 100\%$$

Whereby HHI stands for total household income.

To measure women's and men's respective time burdens of unpaid household and paid work, we can formulate the following time burden indicators, or compare respective leisure times.

• **Women's and men's time burden of unpaid household and paid work**

$$\text{Women's time burden }(in\ hours\ per\ day) = TPW_f + TUW_f$$

$$\text{Men's time burden }(in\ hours\ per\ day) = TPW_m + TUW_m$$

$$\text{Gender division of time burden} = \frac{TPW_f + TUW_f}{TPW_m + TUW_m} \cdot 100\%$$

Whereby, TPW_i stands for time spent on paid work by individual i (and $I = female\ or\ male$), TUW_i stands for time spent on unpaid household work by individual i. These indicators can be compared with pure leisure time indicators to gain a complete picture of women's and men's real time burden:

• **Women's and men's leisure time**

$$\text{Women's leisure time }(in\ hours\ per\ day) = TS_f + TLEI_f$$

$$\text{Men's leisure time }(in\ hours\ per\ day) = TS_m + TLEI_m$$

$$\text{Gender division of leisure time} = \frac{TS_f + TLEI_f}{TS_m + TLEI_m} \cdot 100\%$$

Whereby, TS_i stands for time spent on sleeping and $TLEI_i$ stands for time spent on leisure activities, individual i.

As a matter of fact, in order to assess the *total* time burden of women and men we should also include their time spent on voluntary work outside the realm of the household. This will be added to the above indicators, after having discussed the value of voluntary work in the economy in Chapter 5.

4.10 Time-use data collection

Economic researchers and statistical bureaus apply different methods to collect time use data. Four methods are in use:

- survey questionnaire
- participant observation
- recall interview, or retrospective diary, and
- self-completed current diary.

The choice of method depends on the literacy level of respondents, their time and willingness to respond to a survey questionnaire or keeping a diary, and the researcher's time and budget for data collection, observing her/his participants daily time patterns. Table 4.2 gives an example of a fixed-interval diary format that breaks up 24 hours into time segments. The diary is filled-out by respondents over a particular time period. The categorization of an activity as unpaid household work or leisure takes place ex-post.

Another example of a time use data collection method is the 'light diary method' presented in Table 4.3. In this example, 22 activities are pre-coded and one 'other' is left open. The method can only be used if the livelihoods and main activities are well known to the researcher.

4.11 Policy implications

Because of the invisibility of unpaid household work in National Accounts and the GDP measure, policymakers often assume that there is limitless supply. With the help of time use measures and imputed market wage rates the value of unpaid household work can be made visible. As such, unpaid household work can give input into gender responsive budgets. Gender responsive indicators shed light on the division of unpaid household work, and on the time burden of women

Table 4.2 Fixed-interval diary format

Minutes/Hours	What was your main activity?	What else where you doing at the same time?
0.00		
0.10		
0.20		
0.30		
Etcetera		

Source: Adapted from United Nations (2005: p. 52, Table 3).

Table 4.3 Light-diary format

Activity	0.00-1.00	1.00-2.00	2.00-3.00	3.00-4.00	4.00-5.00	5.00-6.00	Etc.
Sleeping and resting							
Eating							
Personal care							
School (also homework)							
Work as employed							
Own business work							
Farming							
Animal rearing							
Fishing							
Shopping/getting services							
Weaving, sewing, other textile care							
Domestic work (cleaning, cooking)							
Care for children/ adults							
Commuting							
Travelling							
Watching TV							
Reading							
Sitting with family							
Exercising							
Social visits							
Other (specify)							

Source: Adapted from United Nations (2005: p. 53, Table 4).

and men in the economy as a whole. Gender indicators provide useful benchmarks to policymakers to formulate clear objectives; for example, if the aim is to enhance women's economic independence and participation in paid work.

Policymakers should caution for fallacies in effective employment policies and measures. It may not suffice to create pull factors in the paid labor market only; for example, by creating new employment opportunities for women, making sure they have the right education or set of skills, etc. There are three main reasons why these strategies may fail:

I to be employed in the paid labor market is an economic necessity for many women, especially in poor countries. Many women are thus already employed, but often in a home-based or small-scale entrepreneurial activity in the informal sector. Government should install measures to improve women's conditions in the informal sector, for example, by safeguarding their entrepreneurial and ownership rights;

II pull factors may not effectively empower women to overcome the social-cultural constraints faced by them in the household and society that they live in. This may require not only involving a change in men's attitude regarding women's employment outside the home, as well as men's involvement in taking responsibility for unpaid household work, but also a social-cultural change on the unpaid household work including childcare as solely a woman's task (push factors); and

III pulling women into paid employment may not necessarily enable the household to overcome their economic constraints (time, resources) to organize for unpaid household work efficiently and effectively. Women's and men's time cannot be assumed to be infinitely elastic. There are only 24 hours in a day. The professional organization of (affordable) childcare or other household services (fetching water) can relieve intra-household resource constraints, thus freeing-up women's time spent on unpaid household work (push factors).

Different constraints may exist for boys and men to enhance their participation in the paid economy effectively. For example, due to high drop-out rates of young boys from school in Jamaica, they run the risk of being pulled into criminal activities instead of paid employment. In order to formulate gender-responsive policies, economic researchers and policymakers should first identify the gender specific constraints faced by women and men, girls and boys in the paid and unpaid economy in a comprehensive manner.

Furthermore, for economic analysis and policy it is important to know if, in any context, clear gender patterns in the division of unpaid household work exist. Women and men exert different levels of power and influence over household activities and resources. This is important to know when targeting one or the other in policy and interventions. The SIGI is one example of a social institution index that can be used to reflect upon gender relations inside households. For example, microcredit interventions often target women with the objective to enhance their access to capital and income earnings from a small business, although it may ultimately be men who decide about the obtained loan and what investments are made.

Furthermore, women and men may hold different kinds of knowledge over household activities and resources. This is important to know when collecting household survey data on, for example, data on household finances and loans, time spent on unpaid household work, expenditures, housing, food consumption, asset ownership, education and health, and children's economic wellbeing; these may not all be known to one and the same person (e.g. the household head).

Finally in cases of women (or men) performing a relatively greater share of unpaid household work, this may act as a constraint to their participation in the paid economy because the division may be fixed to their gender identities and roles in the economy. As a result, women and men will respond differently to different measures and incentives to push them outside the unpaid economy, or pull them into the paid economy.

Intra-household differences across gender, in interaction with age and status, may result in different levels of individual economic wellbeing. For example, households may choose to invest money and other resources in the education of girls and boys equally, or they may favor one over the other. Another example is when discrimination and abuse may undermine the physical and psychological economic wellbeing of some individuals in the household, and leave other members (relatively) unaffected. The distinction between individual and household economic wellbeing is critical; therefore, we cannot assume that was is good for one household is automatically good for all household members.

Social and economic policies should not overlook the value of unpaid household work to people's economic wellbeing in and outside the household economy. Women's and men's time is not infinitely available; there is a minimum required for unpaid household work, and the reproduction and regeneration of the labor force. This minimum varies across individuals, household type, social-economic category and societies. Social and economic policies should not undermine the efficiency and quality of unpaid household work, but instead think about policies and measures that could strengthen and support the household economy to function well. This will translate in greater benefits to the economy and society as a whole.

4.12 Learning points

- The household is a locus of related individuals whom provide for their economic wellbeing collectively. The household is both a resource agent and social institution.
- The household engages in the production, consumption and distribution of goods and services. The household economy is interconnected with the paid economy in multiple ways.
- Unpaid household work contributes to individual and household economic wellbeing. It also creates positive externalities for the economy as a whole.
- The household can benefit from advantages of scale.
- Power relations shape intra-household processes and outcomes of economic wellbeing. An intra-household model facilitates a gender-aware analysis of economic wellbeing.
- Time use studies shed light on women's and men's allocation of time on unpaid and paid work and on their total time burden. The value of unpaid household work can be measured by assigning a market wage.
- Gender indicators on the division of time and unpaid household work provide important input into defining benchmarks for policy-making and evaluation.
- Social and economic policies should strengthen and support, not undermine, the efficiency and quality of unpaid household work.

4.13 Assignments and discussion points

Discussion point 1 – The division of unpaid work and leisure (20 minutes)
Take a look at the OECD table below (Table 4.4) representing time spent by female (f) and male (m) members of household on unpaid work and leisure in 10 countries. Discuss in groups in which countries gender equality in the division of unpaid work and leisure is highest and lowest. Why do you think this is the case?

Assignment 1 – Calculating gender indicators (15 minutes)
In teams of two, on the basis of Table 4.4 above, calculate the following indicators in three countries of your choice:

Gender division of time spent on unpaid household work
Gender division of leisure time

Discuss how these indicators can inform policy making. What social and economic policies could address the specific gender inequalities observed?

Table 4.4 Time spent on unpaid work and leisure in 10 countries

	Care for household members		Routine house-work		TV or radio at home		Sports		Sleeping	
	f	*m*	*f*	*m*	*f*	*m*	*f*	*m*	*f*	*m*
Canada (2010)	44	21	133	83	99	123	21	32	507	403
Finland (2009/10)	31	12	137	91	111	147	30	37	514	507
France (2009)	35	15	158	98	103	124	24	37	513	506
Italy (2008/9)	23	10	204	57	106	123	25	37	526	520
Japan (2011)	26	7	199	24	140	127	14	17	456	461
Korea (2009)	48	10	138	21	120	125	23	31	462	472
Mexico (2009)	53	15	280	75	71	85	8	15	486	496
New Zealand (2009/10)	44	16	142	76	118	132	15	19	529	522
Spain (2009/10)	42	20	127	76	139	166	12	24	514	510
US (2010)	41	19	126	82	136	162	12	25	522	509
OECD 26	40	16	168	74	112	133	18	26	505	496

Source: OECD (2014).

Discussion point 2 – Time poverty (10 minutes)
Poverty often coincides with a high burden on people's time. Especially, poor women have a disproportionally high time burden. Discuss with the group what factors (social, economic, political) influence poor women's time burden to be disproportionally higher than men's, and higher than the time burden of women whom are more affluent.

Discussion point 3 – The household economy (10 minutes)
Make a list of economic activities taking place in your own household. Categorize them according to production, consumption and distribution activities. Which activities involve the use of market goods and services? Which activities involve the use of public goods and services? Which activities involve the use of household goods and services?

Discussion point 4 – Power and decision making in the household (15 minutes)

Team-up with your immediate neighbor and discuss for each of the listed economic activities, who is in charge of decisions made regarding this activity? Do you think this is the same for a household in Yemen (see Table 4.1). Why/why not? Compare your findings with the Social Institutions and Gender Index (SIGI) website of the OECD to see the breakdown of indicators for Yemen on the country sheet.

Notes

1 The SIGI is focused on developing countries or countries that have undergone rapid development in recent decades. The OECD selected countries for the construction of the SIGI based on the following criteria:
   • non-OECD or non-European Union countries;
   • population of more than 1 million;
   • availability of data on discriminatory social institutions.
2 Variable selection depends on concept operationalization, as well as on data availability.
3 Likert scales measure opinions, feelings and other subjective evaluations on an ordinal scale, usually ranging from 1 to 5, or 1 to 10 and using qualitative labels for each/only the extreme points on the scale. Likert scales have a long tradition of usage in psychology and the social and political sciences.
4 The measurement of voluntary work is addressed in Chapter 5 on Community and Social Groups.
5 We will come back to this issue in Chapter 7 on Economic Performance.

References and suggested further reading

Bloom, S. (2008) *Violence Against Women and Girls: A Compendium of Monitoring and Evaluation Indicators*, Chapel Hill, NC: Carolina Population Center, MEASURE Evaluation.

Cornwall, A., & Brock, K. (2005). What do buzzwords do for development policy? A critical look at 'participation', 'empowerment' and 'poverty reduction'. Third world quarterly, 26(7), 1043–1060.

Ekejiuba, F. I. (1995). Down to fundamentals: women-centred hearth-holds in rural West Africa.

Goldschmidt-Clermont, L. and Pagnossin-Aligisakis E. (1995) Measures of unrecorded economic activities in fourteen countries, in *Human Development Report, Occasional Papers No. 20*, New York, NY: UNDP.

Goodwin, N., Nelson J. and Harris J.M. (2008) Macroeconomic Measurement: Environmental and Social Dimensions, A GDAE Teaching Module on Social and Environmental Issues in Economics, Tufts University Global Development and Environment Institute: M.E. Sharpe.

OECD (2002) *Measuring the Un-Observed Economy. A Handbook*, Paris, France: OECD.

OECD (2014) *Balancing Paid Work, Unpaid Work and Leisure, OECD Gender Equality Home Page, last* accessed on 12th January 2014, Available on-line: http://www.oecd.org/gender/data/balancingpaidworkunpaidworkandleisure.htm

Sen, A.K. (1987) *Gender and Cooperative Conflicts*, UNU-WIDER Working Paper #18, Helsinki, Finland: United Nations University, WIDER.

UNDP (2012) *Gender and Economic Policy Management Initiative – Africa. Short course on Gender-responsive economic policy management. Module 3: Unpaid Care Work*, New York, NY: United Nations Development Programme (UNDP) and Dakar, Senegal: African Institute for Economic Development and Planning (IDEP).

UN (2005). Guide to producing statistics on time use. Measuring paid and unpaid work. New York: United Nations.

UN (2006) *Guide to Producing Statistics on Time Use. Measuring Paid and Unpaid Work*, New York, NY: United Nations, Economic and Social Affairs.

United States Department of Labor, Bureau of Labor Statistics (2012) *American Time Use Survey 2012*, Last accessed on 12th January 2014, Available online: http://www.bls.gov/tus/

World Bank (2013) *World Development Report 2012. Gender Equality and Development*, Washington, D.C.: The World Bank.

5 Communities and social groups

5.1 The position and role of communities and social groups in the economy

The objective of this chapter is to explain the position and role of communities and social groups as resource agents in the economy (Figure 5.1). In mainstream economic analysis, the agency of communities and social groups is often overlooked and rarely modeled. However, communities of people get together and organize in all sorts of social groups: sport clubs, civil society organizations, voluntary associations, professional networks and political associations. Together, they are referred to as 'communities and social groups'. As groups, they make economic decisions about the allocation of resources. Furthermore, they issue rules and regulations, codes of conduct, behavioral principles and norms that shape economic processes and outcomes. Communities and social groups undertake joint activities through voluntary work, networking, political activism and advocacy, and in doing so, share resources. Through community/group membership people also derive a sense of identity and belonging, the value of which cannot be underestimated when considering, for example, people's settlement or mobility patterns. Communities and social groups play an important role in the unpaid economy, for households and individuals to collectively arrange access to and control over resources, organize collaboration and mutual support, and distribute outcomes. But also in the paid economy, communities and social groups play an important role for professional networking, business relations, accessing employment and business opportunities, and career mobility. Women and men participate in communities and social groups to capitalize on their collective strengths, gain access to resources, enhance their voice and empowerment, and arrange mutual support. Communities and social groups also constitute a source of power that individuals alone would never

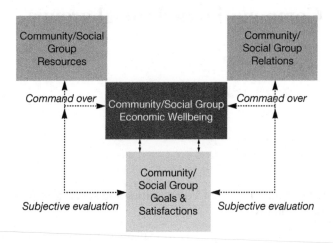

Figure 5.1 Community and social group economic wellbeing.

have. For example, the membership of a political party, protest movement or advocacy group facilitates people to exercise political agency. Gender differences in capabilities, voice and power within communities and social groups influence women's and men's individual entitlements, but are also decisive to group functioning and outcomes. The outcomes of community/social group activities contribute to economic wellbeing (or illbeing), which is influenced by their subjective evaluations of aspired/imposed performance goals and satisfaction or dissatisfaction with the outcomes achieved. Community/social group economic wellbeing refers to the command over resources, relations, and satisfaction thereof, as depicted in Figure 5.1 below.

Box 5.1 Community/social group economic wellbeing

> The economic wellbeing of communities/social groups refers to their command over community/group-level resources, relations, performance goals and satisfaction thereof.

Voluntary goods and services are provided for free or at low costs and replace goods and services otherwise obtained from the market or public sector. A gender-aware economic wellbeing model of the community/social group facilitates the analysis of intra- and inter-group differences in economic wellbeing. Many people invest time in unpaid care work for neighbors, friends and other (near or distant) community/social group members, which involves opportunity costs. In this chapter, the focus

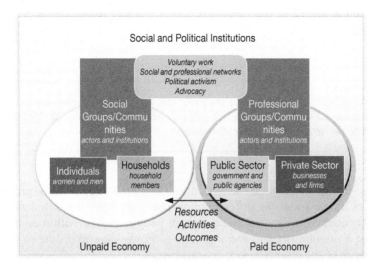

Figure 5.2 The position and role of communities and social groups in the economy.

will be on the value of voluntary work for the economy at large, and how it can be measured. In 2001, the United Nations System of National Accounts (SNA) passed a resolution calling on national governments to record the economic value of voluntary work as part, or alongside their national accounts. Different methods of measuring voluntary work and gender indicators are explained that enable the analysis of voluntary labor by women and men in the economy.

5.2 The community and social group defined

A community is defined as a social unit that connects people through a common set of characteristics, interests, activities and/or shared values. Where the term 'community' is often used to designate a group of people sharing a common geographic, historical or virtual space, the term 'social group' is often used for a group of people that has organized around a common goal or set of values and concrete activities. The boundaries between the two concepts are not clear-cut. Community and social group membership is often set conditional on a list of characteristics, values or goals that members share. Some communities/social groups require an entrance and/or membership fee and a certain degree of commitment and effort to contribute to group activities. In the private and public sector, social groups and communities are known as 'professional' groups or communities, including political organizations, business clubs, alumni associations, and other networks connecting people with a shared interest.

Box 5.2 Community and social group definition

> A community or social group is a social unit that connects people through a common set of characteristics, interests, activities and/or shared values. The two terms are used interchangeably.

This broad conceptual definition of the community/social group leaves ample room for differentiation between professional and non-professional communities and groups of people, but also within each of these. Communities and social groups generally vary according to one or more of the following four characteristics:

• Nature of community/group ties
• Place and space
• Level of homogeneity or heterogeneity
• Temporality
• Level of formality
• Membership criteria

Firstly, the nature of inter-connections or ties that bring people together can vary across community and social group. For one community/group the ties may be religious, for example a community of mission priests, whom share past work experience as missionaries abroad. For another the ties are bound to a shared economic activity, for example a business club of green technology industrials. For yet another the ties are political, e.g. a political party, or social-cultural in nature, e.g. a group of volunteers cleaning the temple grounds and organizing cultural festivities for their fellow community members. Secondly, communities and social groups vary according to shared geographic location or physical space. For example, a city neighborhood group organizing annual festivities and a crime watch service at night recognizes clear geographic and physical boundaries. Whereas, a group of Israeli students commemorating victims of the Jewish Holocaust of World War II may draw on membership from all over the world. With the development of new computer and communication technology, communities and social groups have grown increasingly independent of shared physical spaces and geographic proximity.

Networks of people extend easily beyond geographic boundaries and space nowadays. Thirdly, communities and social groups show diverging levels of homogeneity. Groups can be less or more homogenous in terms of shared characteristics, values, activities, and members' personal characteristics. The collectivity of the group does not warrant unity and consensus within. Communities and social groups know internal processes of collaboration, competition, conflict and contestation, togetherness and strive. Differences in people's capabilities, know-how and power relations shape these intra-group processes. From a gender-aware perspective it is of interest to see to what extent intra-group power differences exist along gender lines, and how these shape group outcomes. Fourth, communities and social groups can be more or less temporal in nature. Group membership can be conditional on a certain age range, for example a group of seniors organizing their own cooking club. Social groups can also exist for a pre-defined period of time. For example, a group of fisher women in Southern Sri Lanka organizing a community saving group for a period of 15 months, whereby 15 members take monthly turns in receiving the collected savings. People are often members of multiple communities/social groups at the same time.

Fifth, the level of formality differs across communities and social groups depending upon formal requirements of being registered with an authority being in place or not. Formal registration may be a pre-requisite of groups to be entitled to access other opportunities and resources, e.g. informally organized self-help groups of smallholder farmers that seek formal registration in order to qualify for government support and access to funding. Sixth and last, communities and social groups may uphold membership criteria by means of which people can be included or excluded from becoming a member. These criteria are often formalized within professional communities and groups of people. For example, political organizations have formalized membership criteria in their rules and regulations, whereas voluntary clubs and neighborhood groups have not. In the latter case, strong social and normative criteria may apply and are used to hold 'members' accountable to their participation and contributions to the group activities.

5.3 Social capital

People like to participate in community and social groups because they expect it will bring certain social, political and/or economic benefits to their human wellbeing. It is often easier to confront a problem collectively than alone. The value ascribed to the returns created by communities and social groups is known as social capital. Robert Putnam's work has been instrumental in advancing the idea of social capital explaining social and economic outcomes (Putnam, 2000). Social capital is defined as the expected individual or collective benefits derived from the collaboration and preferential treatment between individuals and communities/groups. Putnam referred to social capital as the glue that holds societies together. Although social capital is not something tangible, it is associated with having economic value because it builds on inter-personal trust and collaboration. Both are important for social, political and economic institutions to function well and maintain cohesion and stability.

A distinction is commonly made between three forms of social capital:[1]

• *Bonding social capital* denotes the ties that connect people of similar background and beliefs together, for example, between families, close friends and neighbors.
• *Bridging social capital* denotes the more distant ties between acquaintances, classmates and colleagues at work.
• *Linking social capital* encompasses links to people in dissimilar situations outside one's own community, thus giving people access to resources and networks that are not available within their own community/group.

Box 5.3 Social capital

Social capital is defined as the expected individual or collective benefits derived from the collaboration and preferential treatment between individuals and communities/groups. A distinction between three forms of social capital is made: bonding, bridging and linking social capital.

Societies with high social capital have been demonstrated in empirical studies to have lower crime rates, better health and educational outcomes, greater social stability and higher productivity. Social capital has also a function within professional organizations, which is a topic that will be addressed in Chapter 6 on Gender and Firms, Businesses and Entrepreneurs. However, there are also downsides to social capital in the form of (excessive) social control, dislike of outperformance, and high expectations of reciprocity and mutual support.

5.4 Political activism: power and voice in communities and social groups

The economic agency of communities and social groups can transcend the agency of individuals and households because of sheer size. There is power in trust and collaboration, and there is power in numbers. Power determines how resources are distributed. Deepa Narayan, in *Moving out of Poverty*, (Narayan et al. 2011) distinguishes between three forms of power that matter to ordinary people.

These include:

- Power *to* – the capacity to act on one's own behalf, to take initiative, to be autonomous, to influence one's environment
- Power *with* – the power that comes from associating with others, primarily family and friends or in social groups
- Power *over* – the control over people and resources

Being a member of a community/group can give a sense of power, identity and belonging – power *to*. This kind of power gives people inner-strength and belief in oneself to take initiative and persevere in times of hardship. Taking initiative and perseverance have been identified as critical factors to fight and overcome poverty. However, the social capital derived from community or group membership can also undermine an individual's power *to*. For example, women's identities and roles have been, and still are, subservient to men's in many societies around the world. This diminishes women's and girls' voice and power within groups because of a decreased sense of self-worth and autonomy. For example, the decision of a woman in a Northern rural community in Uganda to travel to the market alone, or to attend evening school is conditional on her husband's or father's consent.

Community and social group membership can also give power *with*, because people can associate with others and use their collective strength to achieve a certain goal or gain access to resources and activities that were otherwise inaccessible. It can also enhance political voice, a broader network and leverage to influence political decisions and agenda setting. However, since people of similar social status, background and gender tend to stick together in communities and groups similar to their own, this can limit their associative power because of less powerful social identities. For example, the 'poor sticking to the poor' and 'the rich to the rich', thus perpetuating intra-group power differences and inequalities.

Finally, community and social group membership can give power *over* people, activities or resources. For example power over other groups of people (e.g. Catholic over Protestant; men over women; etc.), or power over a common pool resource or a particular set of private or public goods. The power to exercise control can be grounded in economic possession, political power, social status, and/or cultural and religious relations. Sources of power, or lack thereof can be mutually reinforcing; e.g. economic power can imply social status and political power, and vice versa. Power *over* can also manifest itself as bad power; the power to corrupt, oppress, discriminate, extort, dictate and abuse. Elite capture, favoritism, corruption and suppression skew resource distribution to the benefits of those in power. But even in democratic societies, minorities run the risk of structural marginalization if their interests are not defended by the majority rule.

5.5 Women's and men's participation in communities and social groups

People have different motivations to participate in a community or social group – as far as this concerns a purposeful choice. Their motivations are often related to the perceived benefits generated collectively. Participants seek either individual or collective (family, group) benefits in support of their own wellbeing, or that of other human beings and their physical and natural environment (e.g. maintenance of a neighborhood playground; protection of wildlife). Participation in social groups may also be a source of conflict and strife with family members, or one's peers. Women and men join community/social groups partly for similar reasons, and partly for different reasons that are linked to their gender identities and roles in society and the economy. For example, in the case study on social group participation in rural communities in western Kenya, women and men small-scale farmers both state income benefits as prime motivation of joining the group (see case study in Box 4.3). However, women expect to derive relatively greater benefits than men in terms of access to local decision making. Participation in the community group can enhance women's voice and influence in decision making in community affairs. Men are already included in village governance and decision-making structures through their social identity as heads of family and community leaders.

Communities and social groups show different degrees of self-organization and effectiveness. The degree to which a group is able to reach its goals depends on good leadership and the capabilities and resources that members bring to the group. People have a tendency to stick to people of similar background and/or social-economic or political status. The poor stick to the poor and the rich stick to the rich. This may hamper group effectiveness in those communities and groups with low levels of physical and social capital. This is one reason why women in poorer societies tend to be less powerful than men when organized in groups. Finally, effectiveness hinges on the quality and quantity of bridging and linking connections to other communities and groups, and external people, organizations and networks. Linking social capital is important to mediate access to resources that lie outside the realm of the community/ group.

Box 5.4 Women's and men's perceived benefits of group participation, Samia, Western Kenya

In an on-going research project in Samia County, Western Kenya, among 402 smallholder farmers, we collected data on the self-perceived benefits of community group participation by women and men farmers. The data were collected as part of a baseline survey covering 29 sub-locations and 11 villages. Poverty is relatively high in Samia compared to the rest of the country. The majority of the rural population engages in subsistence level farming, with few capital inputs. Both men and women are engaged in agricultural production, with women performing over 60% of the agricultural labor.

Perceived benefits of men and women (n = 402)		
Benefits	*Men (n = 172)%*	*Women (n = 230)%*
Increased income	**45.3**	**41.4**
Networking	41.3	36.2
Empowerment	37.8	38.9
New skills	35.5	34
Involvement in local decision-making	33.0	28.9
Help on the land (shamba)	20.3	22.4
Access to credit/loans	15.1	20.3
Access to farm inputs and services	15.1	17.7
Sharing of food	18.6	17.7
Help with repairs to house	17.3	12.1
Child care	11.6	10.3

(*continued*)

Box 5.4 Women's and men's perceived benefits of group participation, Samia, Western Kenya (*continued*)

Both women and men farmers in Samia join community groups primarily because they expect benefits to income. Where women then rank empowerment in second position, men rank networking as more important. Although, empowerment appears on men's ranking list and networking on women's list both in third position. Men perceive relatively greater benefits from networking, involvement in local decision-making and help with house repairs, whereas women perceive more benefits in terms of help on the land, access to credit and farm inputs and services.

Source: Pouw et al. (2013).

5.6 Informal rules and regulations

By issuing rules and regulations, communities and social groups manage membership, organize joint activities and decision making within the group. These rules and regulations are mostly informal (or quasi-formal) – meaning that group members expect other members to adhere to them, but without the necessary support of formal law. There may be written (e.g. the internal regulation of a residents' association) and unwritten rules and codes of conduct within communities and social groups. Formal law can work against, alongside (but independent of), in support of, or in combination with informal rules and regulations by communities and social groups. In the latter case, combinations of legal systems and arrangements are also referred to as 'hybrid'.

People are born into communities and social groups, grow-up and may move in and out of communities and groups multiple times over their lifespan. People are member of communities and social groups by nascence, choice or by force. Some communities share a form of livelihood and subsist conditionally on collective access to a natural resource – e.g. a community of pastoralists subsisting by raising livestock on natural pastures. Likewise, smallholder rice farmers in Indonesia who depend critically on the lowland areas of the island economy, whilst indigenous groups in the Amazon subsist on the basis of rain forestry resources, including living space, and the small-scale fisheries communities in the Caribbean need fertile fishing grounds, fish stocks and free landing sites on the beach.

By means of setting rules and regulations, communities and social groups manage access and control over resources. Members of the group whom subscribe to these rules and regulations obtain a right to access and use resources. User rights can either be defined at the community/group level or at the state level (local, national, international) if government recognizes the informal legal system. Community/group rights that have been acquired by custom or local tradition are known as customary rights. Customary rights are grounded in historical and local usages, belonging to communities and indigenous groups inhabiting a particular place. For example, in many African rural economies village communities uphold a customary rights system to control land use and ownership. Community members can use the land for an indefinite period of time and inherit land titles under this system. The customary land system nowadays exists alongside private land rights stipulated in modern law, and grounded in a private land market system. Customary rights are different from pre-scriptive rights, which are stipulated in formal law and refer to rights of individuals independent of their place of residence.

However, legal systems evolve over time and customary systems can become contested in this process. For example, the traditional Hukou system in China prescribes citizenship rights to access education and government services in their original place of residence. With rural-urban migration in China increasing rapidly over the past decades, rural migrants to cities cannot make use of the same public goods and services as urban residents do. Since 2010, these urban inequalities have been increasingly causal to major conflicts and riots in Chinese cities between migrant workers and city governments.

Box 5.5 Customary rights *versus* prescriptive rights

- Customary rights are acquired by custom or local tradition and belong to a community or group inhabiting a particular place or area.
- Prescriptive rights are individual rights, stipulated in formal law and refer to rights of individuals independent of their place of residence.

In the economic analysis of communities and social group economic activities and use of resources, it is important to dedicate special atten-tion to the access and use of common-pool resources, also referred to as common-property resources (CPR). Communities or indigenous groups inhabiting a specific place or area often hold customary rights over com-mon pool resources to derive a livelihood.

A common-pool resource is defined as a natural or man-made resource system (e.g. a forest or communal land) for which it is difficult to exclude potential beneficiaries from using it, because of its size or other char-acteristics. Common-pool resources are renewable (pasture; fish stock;

irrigation system) or non-renewable (coal; oil). The latter are called non-renewable because they take millions of years to form – they cannot be restored in a short period of time. Both renewable and non-renewable common-pool resources stand subject to overuse and congestion. Common-pool resources, e.g. diamonds in the Congo, the Nile River in Egypt, Sudan and Ethiopia, can also be a source of conflict. In countries where this is the case, we speak of the 'resource-curse', or the paradox of plenty. A common-pool resource typically consists of a stock variable, constituting the core of the resource (e.g. water in a lake), and a flow variable, which is a limited amount of extractable fringe units (e.g. fish in the lake). Overuse and congestion occur because of competition over the extractable fringe units. The core resource needs to be maintained and nurtured in order for beneficiaries to be able to exploit the common pool resource in the future. If not, beneficiaries themselves or the future generation may lose the possibility to use a common-pool resource to sustain their livelihood and economic wellbeing. The governance of common-pool resources can benefit from rules and regulations about access and usage to warrant sustainability and/or social equity (within communities). These range from access and user rights, to quota enforcement, protective measures and quality control. Communities and social groups can either self-govern common-pool resources, or government can assign user rights.

Box 5.6 Common-pool resource

A common-pool resource is defined as natural or man-made resource system for which it is difficult to exclude potential beneficiaries from using it, because of its size or other characteristics. A common pool resource typically consists of a stock and flow variable(s) and stands subject to overuse and congestion.

From the seminal work of Elinor Ostrom economists have learned that many (rural) communities engage in a collective form of self-governance to sustain a common-pool resource in the long-run, and/or equally divide resources among community members for social justice reasons (Ostrom, 1990). If members break a rule, or act against the collective interest, this may ensue punishment or community eviction. Sometimes, shared poverty is the only solution to sustain a common-pool resource over time (see case study in Box 5.7).

Box 5.7 Shared poverty in a small-scale fishing community in Southern Sri Lanka

In Rekawa fishing community, Southern Sri Lanka, some 350 house-holds rely on small-scale fisheries for their daily living. Access to the fish-ing grounds, the lagoon and landing sites on Rekawa beach is arranged through a customary fisheries rights system linked to caste. Fishermen go out fishing every day. In the lean season, the community agrees to catch less fish in order for fish stocks to replenish. Income in those months is then derived from women's alternative livelihood activities, such as orna-mental fish breeding, food production, rope-making or a small shop. Poorer households in the community receive food handouts by others, eat-up their savings or resort to the illegal cutting and selling of coral stone. Shared poverty is broadly accepted; breaking the rule and resorting to over-fishing can imply community eviction. This way of living is com-patible with the carrying capacity of the small-scale fishermen's natural environment. Nowadays, this carrying capacity is threatened by overfish-ing of big trawlers, migrant fishers and the tourist industry polluting the lagoon.

Source: Pouw (2012)

5.7 Communities and social groups in the economy: activities, resources and outcomes

Communities and social groups getting together and advocating by organizing voluntary activities, are found in the unpaid economy and paid economy alike (see Figure 5.2). Personal relationships matter both socially and professionally. Where the ties between people in the unpaid economy are mostly social in nature, the ties between communities and groups of people in the paid economy are mostly professional. Although the dividing lines are blurry, for example a network of hospital doctors providing voluntary health services to a poor community. Communities and social groups are actors to which economic agency can be ascribed; they are also institutions because they issue norms and rules, codes of conduct, and behavioral principles. As resource agents, communities and social groups are involved in economic decision making and prob-lem solving. People undertake production and consumption activities together, are engaged in distributing resources and support external ben-eficiaries out of a social concern or necessity. Goods and services used in voluntary work are obtained from the private or public sector, or through gifts or exchanges in kind from other people or communities/groups.

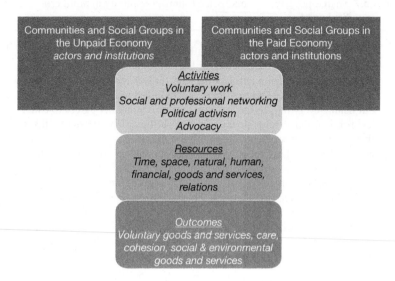

Figure 5.3 Communities and social groups in the economy: activities, resources and outcomes.

The collective can give group members the advantage of scale[2] to access resources (including funds) and networks more easily, organize joint activities more efficiently, and organize advocacy and a collective voice to influence social, political and business agendas more effectively. The outcomes generated by means of community and social group activities are grouped together under "voluntary goods and services" in Figure 5.3. Communities and social groups have intrinsic and extrinsic value to individuals, households and firms. People value communities/ groups because they like to be part of a bigger group and derive a sense of relationship and social identity from participating in that group. People also value communities/groups because of the activities, networks, advocacy opportunities and outcomes provided for collectively. Voluntary goods and services thus provided by communities and social groups contribute to economic wellbeing by satisfying people's needs to live well together as social human beings, and by providing voluntary goods and services, for example in the form of enhanced safety and security in the neighborhood, a business network, or a community-based food distribution system to support poor households and individuals (see Figure 5.4). Communities and social groups are thus included in our comprehensive approach to wellbeing economics on purpose; they play an important role as generators of social capital, social cohesion,

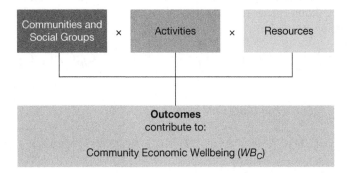

Figure 5.4 Voluntary goods and services contribute to community/social group economic wellbeing.

mutual support systems, and trust, all which are know to contribute to economic stability and wellbeing.

5.8 Modeling community economic wellbeing

In this section, the focus is on modeling the relationship between voluntary work and community economic wellbeing. Again, the Wellbeing Economics Matrix (WEM) presented in Chapter 3 guides the exploration of the two-directional relationship between: a community/social group as provisioner and recipient of voluntary goods and services. Providers and recipients of voluntary goods and services include individuals, households, firms and (local) governments. Community/social group economic wellbeing is also dependent on potential provisionings by the 'rest of the world', but this is left out of the model for the moment, as this will be discussed in Volume II on the Macroeconomy.

Consider the example of a community/social group striving to improve, sustain or protect community/social group economic wellbeing (WB_c). Community/social group economic wellbeing is then the difference between what the community/social group receives from individuals (I_c), households (H_c), firms (F_c), other communities/social groups (C_c), and government (G_c), and what their net savings (SV_c), in the form of goods and services contributing to material $(M_i; M_h; M_f; M_g)$ relational $(R_i; R_h; R_f; R_g)$, and subjective economic wellbeing $(S_i; S_h; S_f; S_g)$ *minus* what the community/social group provides or delivers to individuals (C_i), households (C_h), firms (C_f), other communities/social groups (C_c), and government (C_g), and what their net investments are (N_c), in terms of material (M_c), relational (R_c) and subjective economic wellbeing (S_c).

In the original WEM in Table 3.1 (Chapter 3) this corresponds to the fourth column entries from the left, minus the fourth row entries from the top, being equal to:

$$WB_c = U_c U_j \{I_c; H_c; F_c; C_c; G_C; SV_c\} - U_j U_c \left\{ C_i; C_h; C_f; C_c; C_g; N_c \right\}$$

$$(5.1)$$

or, written in full functional form:

$$WB_C = U_c U_j \{F_c \{M_i \cap R_i \cap S_i\}; F_c \{M_h \cap R_h \cap S_h\}; F_c \{M_f \cap R_f \cap S_f\};$$

$$F_c \{M_c \cap R_c \cap S_c\}; F_c \{M_g \cap R_g \cap S_g\}; SV_c\}$$

$$-U_j U_c \{F_i \{M_c \cap R_c \cap S_c\}; F_h \{M_c \cap R_c \cap S_c\}; F_f \{M_c \cap R_c \cap S_c\};$$

$$F_c \{M_c \cap R_c \cap S_c\}; F_g \{M_c \cap R_c \cap S_c\}; N_c\}$$

$$(5.2)$$

The three wellbeing dimensions can be concretized by means of specifying the variables used in the analysis. For example, in material sense, individuals, households, firms, other communities/social groups and government may provide a certain amount of income $((I_i); (I_h); (I_f); (I_c); (I_g))$ and assets $((A_i); (A_h); (A_f); (A_c); (A_g))$ to the community/social group. This leads to the formulation of five vector variables that can be measured in monetary terms, and which form input into the submatrix (Eq 5.3) of community/social group material wellbeing:

$$
\bullet \quad \text{Community/social group \underline{material} wellbeing} =
\begin{bmatrix}
M_i = \left\{ \begin{matrix} I_i \\ A_i \end{matrix} \right\} \\
M_h = \left\{ \begin{matrix} I_h \\ A_h \end{matrix} \right\} \\
M_f = \left\{ \begin{matrix} I_f \\ A_f \end{matrix} \right\} \\
M_c = \left\{ \begin{matrix} I_c \\ A_c \end{matrix} \right\} \\
M_g = \left\{ \begin{matrix} I_g \\ A_g \end{matrix} \right\}
\end{bmatrix}
\quad (5.3)
$$

In relational sense individuals, households, firms, other communities/social groups and government bring in a set of and/or relational qualities into the community/social group, for example a social support networks

$(SS_i; SS_h; SS_f; SS_c; SS_g)$ and social-political connections $(PC_i; PC_h; PC_f; PC_c; PC_g)$ that form input into the sub-matrix (Eq 5.4) of community/social group relational wellbeing:

- Community/social group <u>relational</u> wellbeing

$$
= \begin{bmatrix} R_i = \left\{ \begin{array}{c} SS_i \\ PC_i \end{array} \right\} \\[2ex] R_h = \left\{ \begin{array}{c} SS_h \\ PC_h \end{array} \right\} \\[2ex] R_f = \left\{ \begin{array}{c} SS_f \\ PC_f \end{array} \right\} \\[2ex] R_c = \left\{ \begin{array}{c} SS_c \\ PC_c \end{array} \right\} \\[2ex] R_g = \left\{ \begin{array}{c} SS_g \\ PC_g \end{array} \right\} \end{bmatrix} \quad (5.4)
$$

Both can be assessed in quantitative terms (number of groups/connections) or in qualitative sense (quality of relationship). In the latter case, a Likert scale technique can be adopted to assess the subjective evaluation of the quality of a relationship on an ordinal scale.

Finally, individuals, households, firms and governments make subjective evaluations on the economic wellbeing of communities/social groups, for example in the form of appreciation/approval $(AP_i; AP_h; AP_f; AP_c; AP_g)$ and cultural pride $(PR_i; PR_h; PR_c; PR_f; PR_g)$. This leads to the formulation of a third sub-matrix of community/social group subjective wellbeing:

- Community/social group <u>subjective</u> wellbeing

$$
= \begin{bmatrix} S_i = \left\{ \begin{array}{c} AP_i \\ PR_i \end{array} \right\} \\[2ex] S_h = \left\{ \begin{array}{c} AP_h \\ PR_h \end{array} \right\} \\[2ex] S_f = \left\{ \begin{array}{c} AP_f \\ PR_f \end{array} \right\} \\[2ex] S_c = \left\{ \begin{array}{c} AP_c \\ PR_c \end{array} \right\} \\[2ex] S_g = \left\{ \begin{array}{c} AP_g \\ PR_g \end{array} \right\} \end{bmatrix} \quad (5.5)
$$

Together, these sub-matrices form the inputs of voluntary goods and service provided for by individuals, households, firms and government to community/social group economic wellbeing.

The above series of equations have made the different sources of community/social group economic wellbeing more transparent by operationalizing the three wellbeing dimensions into concrete concepts and variables that can be measured. They remain, however, purely theoretical relationships. Only after testing the relationships on empirical data, their functional forms can be specified. Moreover, once community/social group (WB_{c1}) can be compared to another community/social group (WB_{c2}) in terms of all economic wellbeing dimensions specified. This will reveal inter-group differences and inequalities in multiple dimensions of economic wellbeing, and tracable to its different sources and origins.

5.9 The value and measurement of voluntary work

Communities and social groups are important loci where voluntary work, social and professional networking and advocacy takes place. In this section we zoom in on the significance of voluntary work for the economy at large, and how it is measured in national accounts. In Section 5.6, it has been explained that people undertake voluntary work on behalf of themselves or others, thus contributing to human wellbeing. Voluntary work also produces economic value by fostering economic growth and stability through social cohesion. Some voluntary income generates income on behalf of others, e.g. voluntary fundraising, selling tickets for a theatre show, providing employment services, etc. Furthermore, voluntary work can also enhance the level of human capital and bring other benefits to society that surpass the immediate economic benefits, e.g. employment training and mentoring, health impacts, social solidarity, political legitimacy, social integration, security, etc. These broader effects of voluntary work are often referred to as multiplier effects. According to conservative estimates the global economic value of voluntary work amounts to over £ 315 billion ($400 billion). More than 400 million people in the world are engaged in some kind of volunteering; per country this varies between 25–40% of the people. Yet, like unpaid household work it goes largely unrecorded in the System of National Accounts.

The first step in measuring voluntary work is to clarify what is regarded as voluntary work and what is not. In this book we follow the definition used by the United Nation Systems of National Account (SNA) and the International Labor Office (ILO). Voluntary work is defined as a service or activity that is undertaken without pay for the benefit of the community, the environment, and persons other than close relatives or those within the household. It is thus separated from unpaid household work that is carried out in the realm of and to the immediate benefit of household members.

Box 5.8 Voluntary work defined

Voluntary work is defined as a service or activity that is undertaken without pay for the benefit of the community, the environment, and persons other than close relatives or those within the household.

Source: International Labor Office (2011).

According to the 2011 *Manual on the Measurement of Volunteer Work* by the ILO, voluntary work has five distinctive features:

1 It involves work; it contributes to the production of goods and services recognized as part of the general production boundary of the economy as defined by the Systems of National Account (SNA)
2 It is unpaid; without pay or compensation, in cash or in kind, although some forms of monetary or in-kind compensation may still be possible (e.g. travel cost, meals, stipend, symbolic gift, training)
3 It is noncompulsory; it must involve a significant element of choice without legal obligation, force or coercion.
4 It involves both direct and indirect volunteering; meaning that the activity relates to other members of society or the environment directly, and organization-based volunteering done for or through nonprofit institutions or other types of organizations.
5 It does not embrace unpaid household work done for members of the volunteer's own household.

None of these features are carved in stone, but they go a long way in explaining the main differences between voluntary work and paid work, unpaid household work, and pure leisure. This kind of conceptual guidance is necessary for statisticians in national statistical bureaus to know what activity or service to classify as voluntary work or not. An example of voluntary work that is considered within and outside the scope of the recommended ILO definition is provided in Box 5.9.

Box 5.9 Examples of voluntary work within and outside the scope of the ILO definition

Within the scope	Outside the scope
Buying groceries for an elderly neighbor	Buying groceries for one's own household
Volunteering as cleaner of the local temple	Cleaning one's own house
Clearing the village road sides	Clearing one's own garden
Assisting an organization create or maintain a website	Participating in a social on-line network community
Driving one's child to hospital	Driving a sick community member to hospital
Providing unpaid legal advice to a civil society organization	Receiving payment for legal advice or assistance

Source: Excerpt from the ILO (2011) Manual on the Measurement of Volunteer Work.

The second step in measuring voluntary work is to assign a monetary value to the hours worked. As in the case of valuing unpaid household work (Chapter 4), there exist multiple methods for doing this, of which two prevail in Satellite Accounts.

The first method measures the *opportunity cost* of the number of hours by assigning the average wage the voluntary would earn in her/his regular job. The idea behind this approach is that the volunteer could have spent the numbers of voluntary hours on her/his job instead. In this case, the underlying assumption is that voluntary work is a substitute for paid work rather than for leisure time. The second method measures the *replacement cost* of voluntary work by assigning the average wage that it would cost to hire in someone for doing the voluntary work. This is the method for calculating the economic value of voluntary work that is relatively more often used by statistical bureaus.

5.10 Voluntary work indicators

The importance of voluntary work to the microeconomy is often underestimated. This is why it is important to also make its value visible and comparable to GDP at the macro-economic level. It is important to recognize women's and men's involvement in voluntary work, and the voluntary goods and services produced by it to better understand their role, decision making and contributions in the economy at large. In countries where voluntary work is measured, differences between women's and men's involvement in voluntary work exist, but not always to a great extent. Overall, women are more likely to engage in voluntary work than men. Variations also exist across the life cycle, socio-economic status, labor market status, and place of residence (e.g. urban versus rural distinctions).

At the national level the participation of women and men in voluntary work can be measured with the following indicators:

National volunteer rate

- $= \dfrac{\text{Number of volunteers in the country in period } t}{\text{Population of the country above the minimum age in period } t} \cdot 100\%$

Volunteer rate of females

- $= \dfrac{\text{Number of female volunteers in the country in period } t}{\text{Female population of the country above the minimum age in period } t} \cdot 100\%$

Volunteer rate of males

- $= \dfrac{\text{Number of male volunteers in the country in period } t}{\text{Male population of the country above the minimum age in period } t} \cdot 100\%$

- At the micro-economic level, women's and men's respective time and value of voluntary work can be assessed by means of the following quantitative indicators.

- *Women's and men's time in voluntary work:*

  Gender division of time spent on voluntary work $= \dfrac{TUW_f}{TUW_m} \cdot 100\%$

  Whereby, TUW_i stands for time spent on voluntary work.

- *The value of voluntary work by women and men:*

  Value of voluntary work provided by women $= TVW_f \cdot MW_f$

  Value of voluntary work provided by men $= TVW_m \cdot MW_m$

  Gender division of total value of voluntary work
  $$= \dfrac{TVW_f \cdot MW_f}{TVW_m \cdot MW_m} \cdot 100\%$$

Whereby, MW_i stands for the market wage value of voluntary work of individual i.

People's engagement in voluntary work implies that their time cannot be assumed to be infinitely elastic. Adding to this their involvement in unpaid household work and the need for leisure time (Chapter 4), it becomes clear that there is more to the economy than paid work alone. The amount of time that people have available to invest in voluntary work is largely dependent on their pre-occupation with unpaid household and voluntary work and paid work. The total time burden of women and men can then be computed by means of the following indicators:

• **Women's and men's *time burden of total work***

Women's total time burden (in hours per day)
$$= TPW_f + TUW_f + TVW_f$$

Men's total time burden (in hours per day)
$$= TPW_m + TUW_m + TVW_m$$

Gender division of total time burden
$$= \frac{TPW_f + TUW_f + TVW_f}{TPW_m + TUW_m + TVW_m} \cdot 100\%$$

Changes in the share of voluntary work can signal the effects of a policy change or economic measures. For example, if paid basic health care services increase in price, some customers will simply pay more, whereas others opt out and instead make use of unpaid care services provided by volunteers. If these services are typically provided for only by women, the price change may eventually have a number of effects:

I   an economic gain for the private health care sector, providing that the number of customers paying extra out-value the loss created by customers opting out;

II an increase in the economic value of volunteer work by women as a share of GDP; and

III an increased time burden of women providing voluntary basic health care services.

If only the first effect was measured, this would lead to a distorted or 'biased' analysis. The example illustrates the importance of considering all effects together, whilst recognizing the value of voluntary work and time invested as an essential part of a gender-aware economic analysis.

5.11 Learning points

- Communities and social groups are resource agents; they produce, consume and distribute goods and services and they define (in)formal rules and norms, codes of conduct, and behavioral principles.
- Community/social group economic wellbeing refers to the command over resources and relations, and satisfactions thereof.
- Social capital holds societies together. A distinction is made between bonding, bridging and linking social capital.
- Community and social group membership can give people power to, power with and power over other people and resources.
- Common-pool resources are often collectively managed.
- Voluntary work, social and professional networking and advocacy are unpaid activities undertaken by communities and social groups in the unpaid and paid economy alike.
- Voluntary goods and services contribute to individual and collective economic wellbeing. Some voluntary work generates immediate income (on behalf of others). Voluntary work also has multiplier effects to the economy at large.
- Voluntary work, like unpaid household work, often goes unrecorded in national statistics.
- The monetary value of voluntary work can be measured either by way of the average wage or opportunity cost method.
- Gender-specific voluntary work indicators shed light on women's and men's involvement in voluntary work, and share of GDP. These indicators inform policymakers and are useful for policy analysis.

5.12 Assignments and discussion points

Assignment 1 – Power to, Power with and Power over (15–20 minutes)
In small working groups of 3–4 participants, read Box 5.4 again. Discuss within the group how Samia women farmers' group participation might enhance their: (i) power to (ii) power with and (iii) power over, people, resources and decision structures in the community. Try to think of good and bad powers.

Assignment 2 – Time to Volunteer (10 minutes)
Ask participants to make a list of all voluntary activities/donations
they engage in, apart from unpaid household work. These can be
activities in the neighborhood or community they live in, or at their
workplace. Ask them to estimate the time involved in each activity, on
average, per year. Collect the data from all participants and calculate
the total time the class invested per year. Round off with a short group
discussion on what motivates people to engage in voluntary activities
in the first place.

Discussion point 1 – Social-Relational Mapping Exercise (20 minutes)
Ask all participants to draw a picture with her/him in the center and
connecting arrows to all communities/social groups she/he is connected
to. Collate all pictures on a big board/the wall and discuss a selection of
them with the group. This exercise helps people to realize that all people
have social ties that matter to them, for social, cultural, political and/or
economic reasons.

Discussion point 2 – Income Generated by Voluntary Work (10–15
minutes)
In groups of two consider this list of voluntary activities and underline
those that generate income (on behalf of others). In what way does the
economy benefit from the other voluntary activities?

*   Volunteering at schools and hospitals
*   Helping out in political campaigns
*   Cooking meals in elderly homes
*   Selling produce from a community garden
*   Caring for sick neighbors
*   Working in shelters
*   Selling tickets for a theatre show
*   Fundraising for international aid
*   Language classes to new immigrants

Notes

1   The work by Michael Woolcock (2001) was leading in making the analytical
    distinction between three forms of social capital.
2   See Chapter 4, Section 4.6 on the advantages of scale in the household,
    which can also be considered as a social grouping.

References and suggested further reading

Coyle, D. (2011) *The Economics of Enough,* Princeton, NJ: Princeton University Press.

ILO (2011) *Manual on the Measurement of Volunteer Work,* Geneva: International Labor Office.

Ironmonger, D. (2002) *Valuing Volunteering. The Economic Value of Volunteering in South Australia,* University of Melbourne: Government of South Australia and Office for Volunteers.

Narayan, D., Pritchett L. and Kapoor S. (2011) *Moving out of Poverty. Vol. 2: Success from the Bottom-up,* Washington, DC: The World Bank.

Ostrom, E. (1990) *Governing the Commons. The Evolution of Institutions for Collective Action,* Cambridge: Cambridge University Press.

Pouw, N.R.M., Peyla-Nagtalon J. and Odame H. (2013) *Social Capital of Smallholder Farmers in Samia District,* Kenya', *UvA/CABE Policy Brief,* Amsterdam: University of Amsterdam.

Pouw, N.R.M. (2012) *Social Well-being in Rekawa Fishing Community,* field report, University of Amsterdam: Governance for Inclusive Development Research group.

Putnam, R. (2000) *Bowling Alone: The Collapse and Revival of American Community,* New York, NY: Simon and Schuster.

UNDP (2012) 'Gender and Economic Policy Management Initiative – Africa. Short course on Gender-responsive economic policy management. Module 3: Unpaid Care Work, New York, NY: United Nations Development Programme (UNDP) and Dakar: African Institute for Economic Development and Planning (IDEP).

Woolcock, M. (2001) The Place of Social Capital in Understanding Social and Economic Outcomes, *Isuma: Canadian Journal of Policy Research,* 2(1): 1–17.

6 Gender and firms, businesses, entrepreneurs

6.1 The position and role of firms, businesses and entrepreneurs in the economy

The purpose of this chapter is to explain the position and role of firms, businesses and entrepreneurs in the economy from a gender-aware perspective and explain how to analyze firm-level economic wellbeing. Although, generally firms businesses and entrepreneurs operate from the motivation of making profits, they may also strive for other social and/or environmental gains. Firms, businesses and entrepreneurs (FBEs) are important resource agents in the private sector of the economy because they produce paid goods and services, create employment and form part and parcel of an entrepreneurial environment in which individual women and men can find employment. They also engage in research and development of new goods and services, thus contributing to technological development and innovation in the economy (see Figure 6.2). According to the International Labor Organization, the *World Economic and Social Outlook Report 2015* (ILO, 2015) points to the economic benefits of increased female participation in the labor forces, resulting in economies being more resilient and less prone to poverty traps. Especially when female and male household members are employed in different sectors of the economy, the household as a whole is more resilient to sudden economic shocks and downturns. The daily management of business operations is embedded within a legal environment of rules and regulations that aim to protect the rights and entitlement of employers and employees. At the meso- and macrolevel of the economy, FBEs are also constitutive of markets and regional, national and cross-border economic activity. This is why the private sector is often seen as the 'driving force' of the paid economy. FBEs sell goods and services for a profit, to customers in local, national, regional or international markets. Customers may include consumers (individuals and households), social groups/communities (networks and associations), other FBEs, and government and non-governmental organizations. Most goods and services produced in the private sector are exchanged for money or other goods and services in markets where buyers and sellers interact. Market exchange requires a legal and institutional environment in which property rights are protected. In legal terms, an FBE can take different forms with varying degrees of personal financial liability and shareholder involvement. Women globally are under-represented in higher-paid jobs within FBEs; where certain business sectors and professions are characterized by gendered divisions. Women are proclaimed to hit the 'glass ceiling' earlier in their career than men, whereby persistent wage inequalities and discounting/devaluing women's labor fail to create the right incentives. Moreover, gender-performed roles and relationships within the household economy also operate as gender barriers to advance a professional career – societal norms and behavioral rules and practices, including gender-influenced women's and men's activities, access to resources and generated outcomes in FBEs. The outcomes of FBE activities contribute to firm-level economic wellbeing (or illbeing, when business is deteriorating), which is partly influenced by the entrepreneurial or stakeholder subjective evaluations of aspired goals and satisfactions or dissatisfactions. Firm-level economic wellbeing thus refers to the FBE's business command over resources, relations, performance goals and subjective satisfaction thereof, as graphically depicted in Figure 6.1 below.

Box 6.1 Firm-level economic wellbeing

> Firm-level economic wellbeing refers to the business command over resources, relations, performance goals and satisfaction thereof.

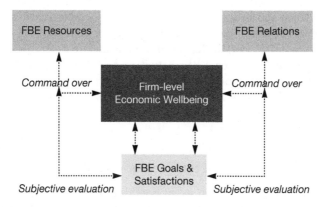

Figure 6.1 Firm-level economic wellbeing.

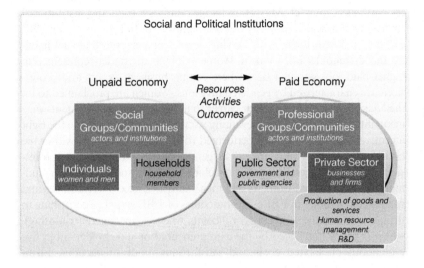

Figure 6.2 The position and role of firms, businesses and entrepreneurs in the economy.

Many women and men in the economy derive an income from being self-employed as micro-, small- or medium-sized entrepreneurs. Entrepreneurs can operate in the formal or informal economy, or in both simultaneously. Social entrepreneurs aim for a social impact, in addition to profitmaking. Home-based entrepreneurs form a special category of entrepreneurs who operate at the interface of the household and the paid economy, for whom the conditions and resources of the household serve as inputs into the economy. In contexts where access to resources is constrained and structural poverty or inequality prevails, it is useful to distinguish between different categories of entrepreneurs. Two types of categorizations relevant for female entrepreneurs are explained. Finally, the relationships between FBEs activities, resources and outcomes in terms of firm-level economic wellbeing are explained, and the steps toward modeling these relationships are disentangled. These form the stepping stones towards possible entries into empirical research on firm-level economic wellbeing.

6.2 The firm, business and entrepreneur defined

A firm or business is defined as an organization that is engaged in the paid production of goods and services to customers. Although, the terms 'firms' and 'business' are used interchangeably, a general distinction is made between the firm having a legal entity, and the business, in more general less formal terms, referring to any profit-making activity, e.g. an informal bicycle taxi service in a small city. In legal terms, a firm can take different forms: sole proprietorship, partnership, limited liability company, cooperative or corporation. In capitalist economies, most businesses and firms are privately owned and therefore part of the private sector. The private sector in Chapter 2 was defined as encompassing all for-profit businesses that are not government owned. In planned economies, most businesses and firms are state-owned, and form part of the public sector. However, public-private ownerships of businesses and firms, under the label of Private-Public-Partnerships (PPPs) can also be found in many national economies.

Box 6.2 The firm and business defined

A firm or business is defined as an organization that is engaged in the paid production of goods and services to customers for profit and other gains. In this book we define a firm as having legal entity, and a business more broadly as any profit-making activity.

Private firms and businesses make a profit by selling goods and services at a higher price than the cost of producing, buying or extracting them. Individual women and men can be an entrepreneur themselves, or work as an employee within somebody else's firm/business. Risk-taking and profit-making behavior are seen as key characteristics of entrepreneurs, but this attribute also results from a male-bias in business literature. A gender-aware perspective draws attention to other entrepreneurial characteristics, including being innovative, capable of multi-tasking, socially well-networked and engaged, and flexible and adaptable to one's (constrained) environment. With more and more women becoming an independent entrepreneur, new concepts and theories are developed to capture these broader notions of 'entrepreneurship'.

Box 6.3 The entrepreneur defined

An entrepreneur is defined as a person who organizes, manages and assumes the risks and rewards for a business venture, including non-monetary business risks and rewards.

In starting-up and operating a private business, women face gendered hurdles and constraints that can tie in with age, race, class, ethnicity and religion. Moreover, in societies where women face many gender inequalities, they often stand subject to abuse and conceit because of their relative independence as entrepreneur. Within the entrepreneurial environment, women entrepreneurs fight against prejudice, discriminatory rules and behavior, and exclusionary practices. As employees, multiple inter-related gender gaps are observed in wages and benefits, training and promotion opportunities, managerial positions, and between professions and sectors.

The degree of risk-taking by entrepreneurs and different contexts varies a lot. Prevailing market conditions, access to information (e.g. on prices) and someone's capacities play a role, next to personal traits and psychology. Risk-taking behavior between female and male entrepreneurs may differ along gender lines because of differences in relative 'fallback positions' – that is a stock of savings, assets, network or alternative options that enable the entrepreneur to cope and recover from an unexpected business setback or loss (Box 6.4). Fallback positions are shaped within a socially institutional environment in which gender identities, roles and relationships (e.g. power differentials) play a role. For example, women in many countries face formal and informal legal barriers to inherit houses and land because of patrilineal inheritance laws. This may prevent them from building up an asset base over the course of a lifetime. Similarly, discriminatory behavior towards female entrepreneurs by bureaucrats and formal administrators also creates barriers to, for example, obtaining a bank loan or getting a business registered. In the case of customary matrilineal laws, inheritance and succession can also pass via the female line, thus excluding boys and men from inheriting property or a cultural position in the family (e.g. as in the case of the Khasi people of North-East India). As a result, the risk-taking behavior of female and male entrepreneurs is nurtured by societal gender norms and internalized by women and men at the individual level. When analyzing the business decision-making of female and male entrepreneurs, therefore, it is important to take possible gender inequalities and differences in fallback positions into account.

Box 6.4 Entrepreneurial fallback position

A stock of savings, assets, networks and/or alternative options that enable the entrepreneur to cope and recover from an unexpected business setback or loss. Entrepreneurial fallback positions tend to differ across female and male entrepreneurs and need to be taken into account when analyzing entrepreneurial decision making.

The Global Entrepreneurship Monitor (GEM) collects data on female and male entrepreneurship. In the early stage of starting up a business, men are more likely to be involved then women. However, in the matured stage, men and women are likely to be equally involved. Yet, stark differences prevail across countries, reflecting gender patterns in labor force participation and cultural differences. GEM data (2012) show that men constitute 52% of entrepreneurs and women 48%. Women dominate the group of entrepreneurs who start up a business out of necessity. These entrepreneurs, often located in developing countries, are also referred to as 'survival entrepreneurs' (see Section 6.6).

6.3 Social entrepreneurship

Mainly because of citizens and action groups claiming human rights to be violated by (big) companies causing environmental pollution, health risks or other dangers to individuals and society, the attention to 'socially responsible business' has grown into an international policy debate. Many young business school graduates seek to become a 'social entrepreneur' these days. Social entrepreneurs are similar to regular entrepreneurs in terms of their profit-seeking goal. But in addition, they aim to have a positive social impact on the society or environment they feel responsible for (Box 6.4). As such, social entrepreneurs integrate a certain degree of social and/or environmental responsibility into their daily operations and longer-term strategies. Social entrepreneurship is seen as an important vehicle for delivering shared value, i.e. value that is shared between the entrepreneur and society.

Box 6.5 The social entrepreneur defined

> A social entrepreneur is defined as a person who organizes, manages and assumes the risks and rewards for a business venture, while also aiming to have a positive impact on society. Social entrepreneurs seek to deliver shared value to society by integrating social responsibility into their daily business operations *ex ante*.

Social entrepreneurship is in theory regarded to be substantially different from Corporate Social Responsibility (CSR). Corporate Social Responsibility is defined as a business taking the responsibility for its negative spillover effects on society or the environment. For example, an oil-extracting industry paying for the costs of cleaning up their water pollution. This is often done *ex-post*, that is, after the business operation has already occurred. Social entrepreneurship assumes an *ex-ante* responsibility, which leads to a different operational design seeking to have a positive impact only. We can thus say that social entrepreneurship and CSR have different points of departure: the social entrepreneur takes 'shared value' as her/his starting point and aims to make a profit. CSR takes profit-making as the starting point and assumes responsibility for (some) negative spillover effects. However, under the umbrella of CSR, other forms of social responsibility by businesses investing in a school, health care or infrastructure with benefits extend beyond their own employees. This makes the dividing line with 'social entrepreneurship' blurry. Also, the dividing line between the broader policy debate on socially responsible business is sometimes unclear. In the scientific debate around socially responsible business and social entrepreneuship, according to some key thinkers in business studies, the two phenomena are indications of capitalism slowly transforming into a new system. Other, more critical thinkers claim that social entrepreneurship and CSR were invented to mask the failures of neoliberal capitalism, creating full employment and sustainable economies. In practice, we see the number of 'social entrepreneurs' growing worldwide, with each putting individual emphasis on social value creation relative to profit making. Whether this is a trend or revolution is currently widely debated. New successful business models have emerged from this (e.g. see the example in Box 6.6), even when targeting low-income producers or consumers.

Box 6.6 The one acre fund

The One Acre Fund in Bungoma, Kenya provides small amount, low-interest loans and offers agricultural education to some 70,000 East African smallholder farmers. It creates groups of 200 farmers who get better prices by buying modern commercial seeds in bulk. The fund also provides crop insurance and strives for farmers working with them to double their profits in a single planting season.

Source: Forbes List of Top 30 social entrepreneurs (2017).

Many women and men worldwide are increasingly attracted to social entrepreneurship, especially young entrepreneurs who are socially or environmentally conscious. In a 2016 Thomson Reuters poll on the phenomenon, it was found that women are particularly attracted to becoming a social entrepreneur because of "the fairer playing field and the higher drive to put compassion over valuation" (Thomson Reuters, 2016). The top-10 countries for women to be working as a social entrepreneur in 2016 are: the Philippines, Russia, Norway, Canada, Malaysia, China, Thailand, Argentina, Hong Kong, and Indonesia.

6.4 Home-based entrepreneurs

Home-based entrepreneurs form a special category who operate their business at the interface of the unpaid household and the paid economy. Many home-based entrepreneurs operate in the informal economy, but certainly not all. Their house or compound, or parts thereof, provides the physical space where most of the business activities (producing, selling, administration, etc.) take place. They combine their business activities with household tasks and responsibilities, interchangeably or simultaneously (e.g. by multitasking), and use household resources (land, food and agricultural produce, energy, furniture, space and equipment/tools) and family labor as 'free' inputs into the production of goods and services. The selling of home-produced goods and services is also often done from the homestead, or nearby. If their customers and markets are located further away, travel or the involvement of traders is required to effectuate sales. Women are well represented among home-based entrepreneurs, since it allows them to combine entrepreneurship with unpaid household activities and resources. In this way, women can be entrepreneurs in places where their mobility is restricted and they are confined to the home/community. Others practice home-based entrepreneurship simply to survive and to maximize or complement income from other sources. Finally, income derived from a business at home may also replace other sources of income in times of the latter being insecure or highly fluctuating (e.g. because of 'high' and 'low' seasons). The income from home-based entrepreneurship helps to smoothen household consumption over time, and thus fulfills an important function from an economic point of view.

Box 6.7 Home-based entrepreneurs

> Home-based entrepreneurs operate their business at the interface of the unpaid household and the paid economy, using paid and unpaid resources and activities household resources and family labor as inputs into the business. Women tend to be well represented among home-based entrepreneurs in many countries due to their multiple gender roles.

Home-based entrepreneurs (HBEs) thus combine paid activities and resources with unpaid activities and resources to produce goods and services that are bought and sold in the private or public sector, or traded in kind in the unpaid economy with other HBEs, households and individuals, and social groups/communities of people. In this way, HBEs bridge the unpaid and paid economy, often times with one and the same product or service. For example, a home-based entrepreneur who cooks meals for the neighborhood public school, caters to local businesses and cooks meals for home consumption.

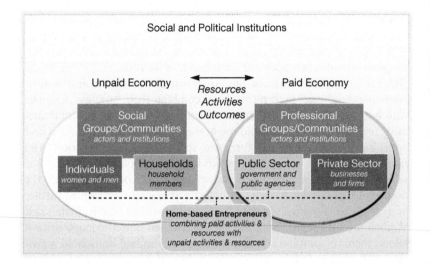

Figure 6.3 Home-based entrepreneurs at the interface of the unpaid and paid economy.

Many HBEs in low-income countries operate in the informal economy, and do not have their business registered under any formal law. This way they avoid taxes as well as compliance to formal rules and regulations, although they may be required to operate with a license or payment to local authorities. Complete formalization is not always an option because of costly and lengthy business registration fees and licensing procedures, or because they lack legal evidence of their properties that could serve as collateral (e.g. a plot of land, a shop). This does not mean that home-based entrepreneurs operate exclusively within the informal economy. Informal home-based entrepreneurs can have several linkages to the formal economy, from which they purchase resources, make use of public goods and services, distill knowledge and information, use infrastructure, and sell goods and services to customers. Home-based entrepreneurs that are formally registered as a private business have to pay taxes and comply with the formal rule of law, e.g. regarding product quality and safe and hygienic production. If they employ other workers in their business, they also need to adhere to rules and regulations regarding labor conditions (e.g. contract, working hours, safety rules). Because of using their house or land as a workspace, however, they can be partially exempted from paying taxes.

6.5 Gender-aware typologies of entrepreneurs

In the international literature on entrepreneurship there are different categories. These categorizations recognize a greater heterogeneity between entrepreneurs, more fit to context. Two such categories are relevant to low-income contexts and gender. The first is the distinction made between 'survival entrepreneurs' and 'growth-oriented entrepreneurs', in line with Berner, Gomez and Knorringa (2012) and Vossenberg (2016). Survival entrepreneurs are entrepreneurs who start a business mostly out of necessity, and who are not prioritizing to grow or expand, unless structural conditions change. Survival entrepreneurs operate primarily in the informal economy, and earn (very) low incomes. Growth-oriented entrepreneurs, on the contrary, are prioritizing to expand their business and earn a (higher) income. In widespread poverty contexts, women are more often survival than growth-oriented entrepreneurs because of their multiple gender roles, gendered risks and lack of opportunities for specialization. Not every survival entrepreneur aims to become a growth-oriented entrepreneur, because this could imply too many risks and uncertainties, incompatibility with the performance of their social-cultural identities, and/or lack of time. There is a large population of women among survival entrepreneurs worldwide, and especially in the informal economy of developing countries. Narrowly fostering women's entrepreneurship by means of improving business skills or market access is, therefore, not a panacea for poverty reduction, as seems often believed by governments and non-governmental organizations.

A second useful categorization from a gender-aware perspective is between different types of home-based economic activities, which are also dominated by female entrepreneurs, following the work of Verrest (2013). This typology differentiates between four types of livelihood and business orientation, based on differences in patterns of organization and contribution to livelihood income, as follows (Figure 6.4):

Type I – vulnerable livelihoods ambition: with a low time input, business operator as main labourer and no others, low technical skills, informal, local market, social networks, low primary and no secondary investments, no designated space and low income but head or on the side, stable at survival level.

Type II – not vulnerable livelihoods ambition: also with a low time input, business operator as main labourer and no others, moderate technical skills, formally acquired, no business skills, local market, social networks, few secondary investment, own funds, space at home, side income, consolidation at security or move beyond.

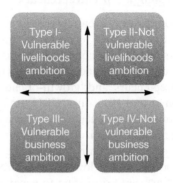

Figure 6.4 Typology of home-based economic activities.
Source: adapted from Verrest (2013), based on Verrest (2007, Chapter 8).

Type III – vulnerable business ambition: with a high input of time, own and additional labour from within household, high primary investment and secondary funding from formal sources, other than own sources, high input technical and business skills, formally acquired, external markets, external designated space, high income, substantial at survival level.

Type IV – not vulnerable business ambition: also with a high input of time, own and additional labour is paid and external, high primary and secondary investment, acquired from formal sources (both) and own sources (primary investments), high input technical skills and moderate business skills, formally acquired, external market, external designated space, higher incomes, consolidation at security and beyond. (adapted from Verrest 2007, Chapter 8).

Women entrepreneurs are generally over-represented in the Type I category, which is related to their multiple gender roles in the unpaid and paid economy, and potential lack of access to resources. Economic policies to stimulate entrepreneurship need to take these different types of entrepreneurs from different settings into account. For example, targeting an entrepreneur with a vulnerable livelihood ambition, with the same policies and instruments as an entrepreneur with a growth ambition (not vulnerable), will most likely not generate similar results. Gender inequalities between female and male entrepreneurs create a further heterogeneity within each category. Women in the poor urban islands of the Caribbean are also over-represented in Type I (Verrest, 2013), and would benefit more from organizing informal saving groups and social support (e.g. child care, shared meals, social transport), than from access to formal bank credit or high-investment innovations with the risk of getting further indebted. Moreover, it should be noted that not everyone wants to become a successful entrepreneur. A home-based economic activity may serve to complement another income, of the same or different member of household, whereby there is no ambition or capability to grow.

6.6 FBEs in the private sector: resources, activities and outcomes

In this section we zoom in on FBEs that are operational in the private sector. This focus helps to explain how their activities, resources and outcomes contribute to firm-level economic wellbeing. Subsequently, we will discuss how PPPs, social entrepreneurs and home-based entrepreneurs also strive to contribute to beyond-firm-level economic wellbeing, or make strategic trade-offs between other wellbeing domains.

FBEs in the private sector engage in the paid production of goods and services for profit and other gains (Figure 6.5). In order to operate they need to manage human capital, which includes the recruitment of employees, their training and professional career guidance, the contractual and institutional arrangements necessary to manage human capital well, and the relations among and between employers and employees. They also provide employment opportunities to the labour

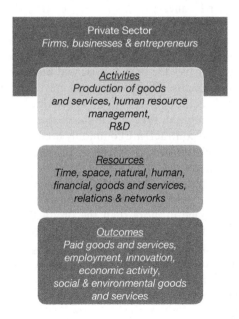

Figure 6.5 FBEs in the private sector: activities, resources and outcomes.

force, and a professional network with other businesses, firms and entrepreneurs through which employers can advance professionally. They create economic activities, which can attract other economic activities within a physical (built) or virtual (digital) environment. A conglomerate of businesses all in one location often attracts other business-to-business suppliers, customers, and public activities and resources (e.g. investment in a digital infrastructure or road network).

For undertaking entrepreneurial activities, FBEs use time, space, natural, human, financial resources and goods and services, and establish professional and social relations and networks. The latter is comprised of both formal and informal networks and professional associations that engage in business and/or social activities with their members. Businesses, firms and entrepreneurs can be operational 24 hours/day, but oftentimes their activities are restricted to a limited number of hours per day (e.g. due to office hours). More or less physical space is needed to carry out business operations. Natural resources can be extracted from the environment and sold as raw commodities (e.g. oil, wood, bauxite) or used as inputs into the production process (e.g. to make coffee, sugar). Apart from the costs of extracting natural resources from nature, businesses/firms do not pay a price for natural resources, unless these are taxed or a license/permit is needed to access them. Raw commodities, goods and services can also be purchased from other businesses/firms in the market, where supply and demand meet. If a business/firm wants to acquire a public good or service, often times a user fee or compulsory tax is paid to a public agency or the government itself; for example, a pharmaceutical company has to pay user fees for certain drug and biologics license applications and supplements. The government may also grant financial resources to FBEs by supporting business activities in the form of a subsidy or a tax exemption. Free gifts in the business sector (i.e. a business gift or a granted contract) are commonly used to leverage business relations, but the distinction with bribes is not always clear. Human resources plays an important role in FBEs with many employees. Their recruitment, training, guidance, compliance, regulation, investment and development require human resource management activities. FBEs thus engage in more than the production of paid goods and services for profit alone. They also create employment, innovation, economic activity and social and environmental goods and services, either in a positive or negative sense. Through a combination of activities and resources FBEs contribute to firm-level economic wellbeing (Figure 6.6), which can thus encompass more gains than monetary and tangible profits alone.

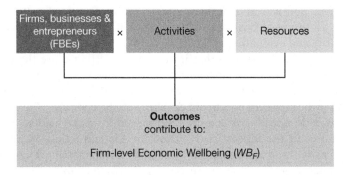

Figure 6.6 FBE goods and services contribute to firm-level economic wellbeing.

6.7 Modeling firm-level economic wellbeing

In this section, the focus is on modeling the relationship between the paid production of goods and services and firm-level economic wellbeing. The Wellbeing Economics Matrix (WEM) presented in Table 3.1 (Chapter 3) guides the exploration of the two-directional relationship between an FBE as provider of goods and services and a profit-making resource agent. Firm-level economic wellbeing also relates to public goods and services (e.g. infrastructure, legal institutions) provided by the government. Last, but not least, FBE activities, resources and outcomes and thus firm-level economic wellbeing are also connected to the 'rest of the world', but this is left out of the model for the moment and will be treated in Volume II on the Macroeconomy.

Consider the example of an FBE striving to improve, sustain or protect firm-level economic wellbeing (WB_F), in particular material gains by profit-making, but possibly also non-material gains, such as good customer relations, and a solid business reputation or brand name. The FBE provides (sells, rents/leases, donates/dumps) goods and services to individuals (F_i), households (F_h), communities/social groups (F_c), other FBEs (F_f), the government (F_g) and its net savings (SV_f), by means of which it builds up a 'stock' of assets, business relations and recognition and satisfaction of past performances, which impact the three dimensions of firm-level economic wellbeing in the material (M_f), relational (R_f) and subjective sense (S_f). As inputs into the production of goods and services, the FBE can obtain (hires, buys or extracts) labour and resources $(M_i; M_h; M_c; M_f; M_g)$ from individuals (I_f), households (H_f), communities/social groups (C_f), other FBEs

(F_F), the government (G_f), and its net investments (N_f), drawing upon its social, political and business network $(R_i; R_h; R_c; R_f; R_g)$, and within a context of business good- or badwill, goals and performance indicators and evaluations $(S_i; S_h; S_c; S_f; S_g)$.

It should be noted here that in regards to FBEs we use the terms 'provides' and 'obtains' instead of the customary 'sells' and 'buys', because of our broader perspective on business activities, which may extend into the paid and unpaid domains of the economy. For example, FBEs do not always acquire their inputs from the paid economy or pay for all the inputs used – think of the extraction of natural resources without reinvesting in nature, or compensating a community depending on these resources, or of forced labour. Likewise, FBEs, and especially social entrepreneurs, may provide goods and services to certain groups of people/communities for free, or at below-market prices. For example, a company that donates money to a city neighborhood to fund an artistic project in the park, or a lawyer who provides legal services at reduced rates to migrants.

In the WEM in Table 3.1 (Chapter 3), the above corresponds to the third column entries from the left, minus the third row entries from the top, being equal to:

$$WB_F = U_j U_f \left\{ F_i; F_h; F_c; F_f; F_g; SV_f \right\} - U_f U_j \{ I_f; H_f; C_f; F_f; G_f; N_f \} \quad (6.1)$$

or, written in full functional form:

$$WB_F = U_j U_f \{ F_i \left\{ M_f \cap R_f \cap S_f \right\}; F_h \left\{ M_f \cap R_f \cap S_f \right\}; F_c \left\{ M_f \cap R_f \cap S_f \right\};$$
$$F_f \{ M_f \cap R_f \cap S_f \}; F_g \left\{ M_f \cap R_f \cap S_f \right\}; SV_f \} - U_f U_j \{ I_f \{ M_i \cap R_i \cap S_i \};$$
$$H_f \{ M_h \cap R_h \cap S_h \}; C_f \{ M_c \cap R_c \cap S_c \}; F_f \{ M_f \cap R_f \cap S_f \}; C_f \{ M_c \cap R_c \cap S_c \};$$
$$F_f \left\{ M_f \cap R_f \cap S_f \right\}; G_f \left\{ M_g \cap R_g \cap S_g \right\}; N_f \}$$

$$(6.2)$$

The three wellbeing dimensions can be concretized by means of specifying the variables used in the firm-level economic wellbeing analysis. For example, in a material sense, FBEs receive income $((I_i); (I_h); (I_c); (I_f); (I_g))$ and assets $((A_i); (A_h); (A_c); (A_f); (A_g))$ from individuals, households, communities/social groups, other FBEs, and government by selling their goods and services. This leads to the formulation of five vector variables that can be measured in monetary terms, and which form input into the sub-matrix (Eq 6.3) of firm-level material wellbeing:

$$\bullet \quad \text{Firm-level material wellbeing} = \begin{bmatrix} M_i = \begin{Bmatrix} I_i \\ A_i \end{Bmatrix} \\ M_h = \begin{Bmatrix} I_h \\ A_h \end{Bmatrix} \\ M_c = \begin{Bmatrix} I_c \\ A_c \end{Bmatrix} \\ M_f = \begin{Bmatrix} I_f \\ A_f \end{Bmatrix} \\ M_g = \begin{Bmatrix} I_g \\ A_g \end{Bmatrix} \end{bmatrix} \quad (6.3)$$

In a relational sense individuals, households, communities/social groups, other FBEs and government bring in a set of qualities related to the FBE, for a well-networked labour force *(NLF$_i$; NLF$_h$; NLF$_c$; NLF$_f$; NLF$_g$)* and political cohesion *(PC$_i$; PC$_h$; PC$_c$; PC$_f$; PC$_g$)* that form input into the sub-matrix (E.6.4) of firm-level relational wellbeing:

$$\bullet \quad \text{Firm-level relational wellbeing} = \begin{bmatrix} R_i = \begin{Bmatrix} NLF_i \\ PC_i \end{Bmatrix} \\ R_h = \begin{Bmatrix} NLF_h \\ PC_h \end{Bmatrix} \\ R_c = \begin{Bmatrix} NLF_c \\ PC_c \end{Bmatrix} \\ R_f = \begin{Bmatrix} NLF_f \\ PC_f \end{Bmatrix} \\ R_g = \begin{Bmatrix} NLF_g \\ PC_g \end{Bmatrix} \end{bmatrix} \quad (6.4)$$

Both can be assessed in quantitative terms (number of connections) or in qualitative sense (quality of relationship). In the latter case, a Likert scale technique can be adopted to assess the subjective evaluation of the relationship quality on an ordinal scale.

Finally, individuals, households, communities/social groups, firms and government provide subjective evaluations to the FBE; for example, in the form of brand loyalty *(BL$_i$, BL$_h$; BL$_c$; BL$_f$; BL$_g$)* and positive CSR ratings *(CSR$_i$; CSR$_h$; CSR$_c$; CSR$_p$; CSR$_g$)*. This leads to the formulation of a third sub-matrix (Eq 6.5) of firm-level subjective wellbeing:

- Firm-level subjective wellbeing =
$$
\begin{bmatrix}
S_i = \left\{ \begin{array}{c} BL_i \\ CSR_i \end{array} \right\} \\
S_h = \left\{ \begin{array}{c} BL_h \\ CSR_h \end{array} \right\} \\
S_c = \left\{ \begin{array}{c} BL_c \\ CSR_c \end{array} \right\} \\
S_f = \left\{ \begin{array}{c} BL_f \\ CSR_f \end{array} \right\} \\
S_g = \left\{ \begin{array}{c} BL_f \\ CSR_f \end{array} \right\}
\end{bmatrix}
\tag{6.5}
$$

The above series of equations have made the different sources of firm-level economic wellbeing more transparent by operating the three wellbeing dimensions into concrete concepts and variables that can be measured. They remain, however, purely theoretical relationships. Only after testing the relationships on empirical data can their functional forms be specified. Moreover, firm-level *(WB$_{f1}$)* can be compared to another firm *(WB$_{f2}$)* in terms of all economic wellbeing dimensions specified. This will reveal inter-firm differences and inequalities in multiple dimensions of economic wellbeing, tracing back to its different sources and origins.

6.8 Measuring gender targets within FBEs

Within FBEs, gender targets can be defined as part of the business mission statement and goals. The underlying objective of setting gender targets can be to overcome gender differences and inequalities in employment (type and level), representation and wage income. Moreover, both intrinsic and instrumental value is assigned to creating gender diversity in the workplace, as this would contribute to improved FBE performance. Three prime drivers for enhancing gender equality within FBEs and other types of organisations include: (i) the ability to make better decisions and create innovative solutions through a more flexible and creative organisation; (ii) attracting and retaining a highly talented workforce; and (iii) enhanced organizational reputation (GoA, 2013). An increasing number of countries in the world have workplace gender equality acts in place, and some FBEs make this an integral part of their CSR strategy. In order to provide inputs for assessment and monitoring of gender targets within FBEs, two examples for measurement are given. One is computing a Gender Diversity Index at the workplace level, and the second example is a method to assess gender pay gaps.

Gender diversity in the workplace is defined as a heterogenous workforce in terms of women and men, at different levels of operation. Within FBEs there may well be an equal number of women and men working, but that doesn't mean there is gender diversity at all job levels. Job level (scales/categories) can be deployed to compute the shares of female and male workers at each level. Independent of educational performance indicators, women do not seem to reach top management positions as often as their male counterparts do. This can be related to gender barriers and constraints over and beyond education, access to networks, incompatibility with other tasks, time and resources. But it can also relate to internalized gender performances in the form of less aspirational behaviour and motivational attitudes.

Box 6.8 Gender diversity in the workplace

Gender diversity in the workplace implies a heterogeneous workforce, in terms of women and men, at different operational levels.

Globally, there is a minority of women being represented at higher, managerial positions, but this varies a lot per sector and size of FBE. For example, as illustrated in Figure 6.7, by comparing women's participation rate in the workforce to the proportion of women on boards in Auralia to 16 other countries in the world. Women's board representation is highest in Norway, where it reaches above 40 percent and where it is not strongly correlated to women's participation rate in the paid labour market.

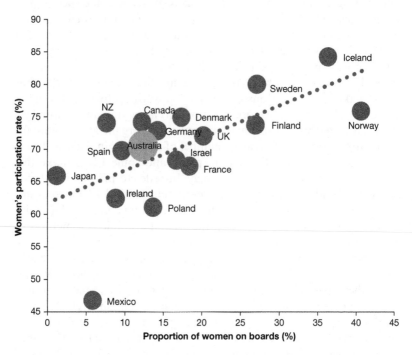

Figure 6.7 Workforce participation and board representation of women in Australia and other countries.

Also, in Europe and the United States the case for gender diversity at the workplace, especially in managerial positions, is compelling as can be read in Box 6.9 below.

Box 6.9 Slow progress towards gender diversity in top management

Progress towards equal representation of women and men in top management is slow. For example, in Western Europe, 17 percent of executive committee members are women, and 32 percent of corporate board members are women for companies listed in major market indexes. This compares to 17 percent in the United States for executive committees, and a little under 19 percent for boards.

Source: McKinsey (2016).

The Gender Diversity Index is computed as follows:

Gender Diversity Index (GDIV)

$$= \frac{\text{Number of female workers, at level } 1..n}{\text{Number of total (female and male) workers, at level } 1..n} \times 100\%$$

(6.6)

The second method for assessing and monitoring gender inequalities within FBEs is the Gender Pay Gap index. The gender pay gap is the average difference between women's and men's total income, adjusted for all external factors that explain income differences, including education, working time interruptions, and years of working experience. The gender

Box 6.10 Gender pay gap

> The gender pay gap is the average difference between women's and men's total income, adjusted for all external factors that explain income differences.

pay gap can be computed at multiple levels: business, sector, and national and global.

- At FBE level, the computation of the Gender Pay Gap index is as follows:

$$\text{Gender Pay Gap Index (GPG)} = \sum_{ij} \frac{\left(W_{ij}^f - W_{ij}^m\right)}{n_{ij}} \times 100\%$$ (6.7)

where W^f stands for wage income of female workers, W^m for wage income of male workers, for every *i*-th person in job level *j*, and *n* stands for total number of workers, and sigma for sum.

At the global level it allows for comparison across countries. For example, the global gender pay gap in 2015, which was based on data coming from 145 countries, ranged inbetween 22 and 52 percent (WEF, 2015). The gender pay gap is predominantly explained by gender inequalities in political and economic empowerment, whereas previous gender inequalities in education and health have become much smaller over recent decades.

6.9 Learning points

- Firm-level economic wellbeing refers to the business command over resources, relations, goals and satisfaction thereof.

- A firm or business is defined as an organization that is engaged in the paid production of goods and services to customers for profit and other gains.
- An entrepreneur is defined as a person who organizes, manages and assumes the risks and rewards for a business venture, including non-monetary business risks and rewards.
- A social entrepreneur is defined as a person who organizes, manages and assumes the risks and rewards for a business venture, whilE also aiming to have a positive impact on society.
- Entrepreneurial fallback positions differ between female and male entrepreneurs.
- Home-based entrepreneurs operate their business at the interface of the unpaid household and the paid economy.
- Gender-aware typologies of entrepreneurship are better suited to capture the variety of female and male entrepreneurs in different contexts.
- The paid production of goods and services contribute to firm-level economic wellbeing.
- Gender diversity at the workplace implies a heterogeneous workforce, in terms of women and men, at different operational levels.
- The gender pay gap measures the average difference between women's and men's total income, adjusted for all external factors that explain income differences.

6.10 Assignments and discussion points

Assignment 1 – Entrepreneurial trade-offs (20 minutes)
In small working groups of 3–4 participants, discuss the case of a small, informal sector survival entrepreneur in Quetzaltenango, Guatemala, who sells handmade fabrics on the roadside and also takes care of three children as a single parent. Selling along the roadside only gives a small price for the fabrics, but has the advantage of being close to the homestead and no fees are charged. Selling fabrics at the local marketplace in the city centre would give a better price, but would also involve costs for transportation and a market fee. Discuss within the groups: (i) how this small entrepreneur could enhance profits, while keeping these multiple trade-offs in mind? (ii) would these trade-offs be different for a female or male survival entrepreneur, and why/why not?

Discussion point 1 – Social entrepreneurship (10 minutes)
Ask participants to make a list of all social entrepreneurs/enterprises they know of, in their own town, country or internationally. Ask them to specify the distinguishing criteria of each for being qualified as a 'social entrepreneur'? How many of them strive for a social impact? How many of them

strive for an environmental impact? Discuss with the group that 'social entrepreneurship' is a contested concept, with varying practices. Discuss with the participants if they expect to see the number of social entrepreneurs to increase in the nearby future, and what could be some reasons why?

Assignment 2 – Firm-level economic wellbeing (10 minutes)
Ask all participants to team-up with their nearest neighbor and ask them to discuss determinants of failure or success of a multi-national company that is selling sneakers on the global market, which are designed in the United States but produced in a low-income country. The discussion should try to cover aspects that go beyond the making of profits only. Indicate per determinant mentioned, whether this would fall under the (i) material (ii) social-relational or (iii) subjective dimension of firm-level economic wellbeing.

Discussion point 2 – Setting gender targets for FBEs (15–20 minutes)
Consider together the example of a leading, well-known FBE in your country; let the participants choose one. Discuss together what type of *gender-aware targets* the FBE could include in her business goals and strategy in order to boost economic performance, attract and retain highly skilled and motivated employees, and improve its reputation as a gender-diverse employer. Discuss what *gender indicators* could be formulated for each target. Try to be creative in proposing new indicators. How can these targets be monitored over time?

References and suggested further reading

Berner, E., Gomez, G. and Knorringa, P. (2012) Helping a large number of people become a little less poor: the logic of survival entrepreneurs. *European Journal of Development Research, 24*(3), 382–396.

Driver, M. (2012). An interview with Michael Porter: social entrepreneurship and the transformation of capitalism. *Academy of Management Learning & Education, 11*(3), 421–431.

GoA (2013) *How to set gender diversity targets.* Government of Australia. Sydney: Workplace Gender Equality Agency. Available on-line: https://www.wgea.gov.au/sites/default/files/SETTING-GENDER-TARGETS-Online-accessible.pdf

Vidal, C.A., Rusca, M. Zwarteveen, M. Pouw N. and Schwartz K. (2017). Occupational genders and gendered occupations: the case of water provisioning in Maputo, Mozambique. *Gender, Place and Culture* (in print). DOI available: dx.doi.org/10.1080/0966369X.2017.1339019

ILO (2015) *World Economic Outlook 2015.* Geneva, Switzerland: International Labor Organization.

McKinsey (2016) *Women in the Workplace 2016.* London,UK: McKinsey Company.

Oostendorp, R.H. (2004). Globalization and the gender wage gap. *World Bank Economic Review 23*(1): 141–161.

Porter, M.E. and Kramer M.R. (2011). The big idea: creating shared value. *Harvard Business Review, 89*(1), 2.

Seguino, S. (2003). Taking gender differences in bargaining power seriously: equity, labor standards, and living wages. MPRA paper, Berlington, VT: University of Vermont.

Soto, de H. (2003). *The Mystery of Capital: Why Capitalism Succeeds in the West and Fails Everywhere Else*, New York, NY: Basic Books.

Terjesen, S. A., & Lloyd, A. (2015). The 2015 female entrepreneurship index. Global Entrepreneurship and Development Institute. And also: Buvinic, M., Furst-Nichols, R. and Pryor, E.C. (2013) A roadmap for promoting women's economic empowerment. United Nations Foundation and ExxonMobil Foundation.

Thomson Reuters (2016). *Where are Women Most Actively Leading Social Enterprises?* Tang A. and Yi B.L. (eds), London, UK: Thomson Reuters Foundation.

Thorpe, A., Pouw, N., Baio, A., Sandi, R., Ndomahina, E. T., and Lebbie, T. (2014). "Fishing Na Everybody Business": women's work and gender relations in Sierra Leone's fisheries. *Feminist Economics, 20*(3), 53–77.

Verrest, H. (2007). *Home-Based Economic Activities and Caribbean Urban Livelihoods: Vulnerability, Ambition and Impact in Paramaribo and Port of Spain*. Amsterdam, the Netherlands: Amsterdam University Press.

Verrest, H. (2013). Rethinking microentrepreneurship and business development programs: vulnerability and ambition in low-income urban Caribbean households, *World Development 47*: 48–70.

Vossenberg, S. (2016) *Gender-Aware Women's Entrepreneurship Development for Inclusive Development in Sub-Saharan Africa*. Available on-line: http://Includeplatform.net/wp-content/uploads/2016/01/INCLUDE-GRF-Vossenberg-Gender-Aware-Women's-Entrepreneurship-Development.pdf

WEF (2015) *The Global Gender Gap Report 2015*. Geneva, Switzerland: World Economic Forum. Available on-line: http://www3.weforum.org/docs/GGGR2015/cover.pdf

7 A different conception of economic performance

7.1 Broadening the debate

In this final chapter we will learn about alternative ways to evaluate the overall performance of the economy from a more inclusive and gender-aware perspective, and why this matters, and to whom. This broader understanding of economic performance forms part and parcel of our gender-aware approach to the Microeconomy as put forward in this book. The purpose of this chapter is to demonstrate how viewpoints on economic performance influence systems of measurement and indicators. The total amount of goods and services produced, Gross Domestic Product (GDP) is widely used to measure the size of a national economy in terms of its productivity, and make comparisons across countries. The growth rate of GDP is therefore seen as a key indicator of economic performance. In Chapter 3 we questioned the primacy of the GDP measure, since it neither captures the value of unpaid household work (Chapter 4) nor the value of voluntary work and social and natural capital (Chapter 5). Moreover, although economic growth is important for generating resources for new investments, the quality, distribution and stability of growth matters at least as much to people in the economy. Economic growth can bring benefits to some, but have negative consequences for others and the natural environment. People may experience economic security and the availability of jobs and livelihood resources as more immediate determinants of quality of life than aggregate GDP. We will therefore move beyond the traditional efficiency-equality dichotomy and identify complementary economic performance indicators to GDP growth that do more justice to production in the unpaid economy. This conveys our gender-aware perspective at the macro-economic level. Moreover, as explained in Chapter 3, social inequity and environmental sustainability are raised as critical themes that cannot be overlooked when evaluating economic performance from a more inclusive perspective. This requires the recognition and valuation of intangible assets as compounding factors to economic performance. We will therefore introduce a number of alternative performance indicators that can be used to assess society's progress in multiple dimensions. These indicators are useful to capture some of the externalities of economic growth that go otherwise unrecorded in economic analysis and policy evaluation.

7.2 Economic performance

Economic performance is the assessment of an economy in relation to how it functions and what outcomes it produces to the people who constitute the economy, and the environment in which it is embedded. Economic performance is, in essence, a measure of success for an economy to deliver on its prime functions. What these prime functions are, what outcomes are produced, and for whom or what is part of a long-standing debate in the field of economics.

Box 7.1 Economic performance

> Economic performance is the assessment of an economy in relation to how it functions and what outcomes it produces to the people who constitute the economy, and the environment in which it is embedded.

Historically, *efficiency* has been the theoretical and conceptual criterion in economics to assess whether an economy is functioning in an optimal manner. The reasoning behind this is an efficient economy precludes the highest amount of total output that can be produced at any given point in time. An economy is said to be more efficient, and thus performing better than another economy, when it can produce more goods and services without using more resources. This is how Gross Domestic Product (GDP) – being the total market value of all final goods and services produced in an economy – became the dominant measure of economic performance. Before turning to a discussion on the GDP as an indicator of economic growth, we first explore the discourse behind the efficiency argument in economics in order to understand the importance assigned to it in neoclassical economic growth theory.

Different definitions of efficiency prevail in the economic literature; sometimes efficiency is defined as a broad term and sometimes in a more narrow sense. For example, economic efficiency is often defined as the situation in which:

• No one can be made better off without making someone else worse off (Pareto efficiency)

- No extra output can be obtained without increasing input.
- Resources are utilized as to maximize total production of goods and services.

In a narrow economic sense, efficiency refers to the cost-efficiency of production. It proceeds from the underlying objective of profit maximization by firms in a capitalist system, when costs are minimized relative to the benefits of production. The advantage of defining efficiency as cost-efficiency is that the concept becomes measurable in monetary terms. If cost and benefit data are available, efficiency can even be calculated as the most optimum point at which production generates the highest marginal benefits and the lowest marginal costs. This optimum point can be objectively assessed. However, the choice to define efficiency in terms of the cost-efficiency of production only, remains in itself a subjective and value-laden decision.

But measuring the cost-efficiency of production in itself is not without difficulties. One can imagine that cost-benefit analysis is quite feasible at the level of one production process, firm or organization, but it is much more difficult to achieve for a cluster of firms or organizations, let alone for an entire economy. At these higher levels of aggregation, other costs and benefits start to influence the production function (positively or negatively) – e.g. lower transportation costs due to infrastructure being available or higher procurement costs due to inefficient institutions. Furthermore, efficiency in the sense of cost-efficiency is a rather limited judgment tool that can overrule other qualities of the production process, such as 'waste-free' production or 'socially responsible' use of resources. Cost-efficiency can be accompanied by externalities, such as costs or benefits to people or the environment that did not choose to incur them. For example, when a manufacturer causes water pollution that incurs a cost to society because it needs to be cleaned up. To pursue cost-efficiency as the only way to manage production processes can easily turn into an economic vice, rather than a virtue.

Box 7.2 Economic externality

An economic externality is a cost or benefit that affects people in society or the environment that did not choose to incur that cost or benefit.

In this book, we prefer to define efficiency in a broad sense, so that it is more appealing to our intuition. Efficiency then refers to the general ability to utilize resources without (or a minimum of) material waste and immaterial resources, such as money, assets, human capital, time, space, natural resources and energy. This definition has greater appeal to the everyday economic behavior of economic agents. Efficiency can also be seen as an economic virtue that guides people to a balanced and responsible use of resources, without dictating them to a strict (and rather impossible) cost-benefit analysis for each and every economic decision. This leaves ample room for combining the efficiency criterion with other evaluation criteria to assess economic performance in a meaningful way.

Box 7.3 Efficiency broadly defined

> Efficiency broadly refers to the ability to utilize resources without wasting resources, including money, time and energy.

Where we can imagine that most economic agents strive for efficiency in utilizing resources, some do so more than others, and for different reasons. To private sector firms cost-efficiency is considered necessary to maximize profits and be competitive; cost-benefit analysis is enshrined in their day-to-day business management. But likewise, and increasingly so, we find private firms and social entrepreneurs adopting other, societal rules and norms as well – e.g. green production and social responsibility (see also Chapter 6). Individuals and households may well strive for efficient use of resources, but without doing cost-benefit calculations at the kitchen table all the time. The same applies to communities and social groups. They commonly have a system of resource management in place according to a practical or normative community/group rule or norm (e.g. equal sharing; protecting the poorest; sustainable use) that complements or replaces the efficiency rule. Government agencies and public organizations may also commit to efficiency, but do not always strictly adhere to it due to redistributive principles. In the case of public sector corruption and kleptocratic elites, individual profit maximization supersedes collective interests and can even undermine cost-efficiency.

Efficiency thus may constitute an important rule of thumb to measure economic performance in the economy at one level, but it clearly works in combination or alteration with other rules and norms at another level, where it meets counter-forces and diverging interests. Here we proclaim that 'efficiency' is but one criterion of how well the economy functions. Another criterion may be social equity. Equity refers to the idea of 'fairness' in economic opportunities and/or outcomes. In relation to the Millennium Development Goals, equity refers to the provisioning of basic income, goods and services to all citizens, so that no one suffers from poverty. The topic of equity was high on the agenda of economists and policymakers in the 1970s when many Northern American and Western European countries were shifting towards a welfare state regime. Economic equality was pursued in diversified ways by implementing a range of redistributive mechanisms in the economic system permanently, including such things as a progressive income tax, social security, pension schemes, health insurance and subsidized education. High inequality is generally seen to undermine economic growth through the enhancement of economic instability, structural poverty and conflict risks. However, what is considered 'high' or 'low' inequality remains a subjective judgment.

Box 7.4 Equity

Equity, or economic equality refers to a sense of 'fairness' in economic opportunities and/or outcomes.

The Gini index is a widely used measure to assess the dispersion of incomes in a national economy. This measure is adjusted for taxes and transfers to capture the different redistributive welfare effects in cross-country comparisons. Economic equality is gaining more attention from economists again these days, in view of the world-wide trend of inequality increasing since the 1980s, especially between people living in the same country.[1] In general, income inequality tends to be lower in countries where income tax is high and social redistributive policies and mechanisms are in place.

One example of this equalizing effect is presented in Table 7.1 below. Here we can see that in countries with high top income tax rates and a low income threshold, e.g. in Denmark, Sweden, Belgium, The Netherlands, Finland and Norway, income inequality as measured by the Gini coefficient is much lower compared to countries with lower top income tax rates and high income thresholds, such as the US, Korea and Spain. Despite redistribution taking place in an economy, there may exist other non-income obstacles and constraints to accessing public goods and services; for example, geographic and social-cultural and gender barriers, which prevent certain (groups of) people accessing publically provided goods or services. For example, in 2010 in Afghanistan, 54% of school-aged children were enrolled in school;

Table 7.1 Top income tax and income inequality as measured by Gini, by country

Country	Top Income Tax Rate 2013	Income Threshold 2013	Income inequality (Gini)
Denmark	60%	$54.9K	24.8% (2011)
Sweden	57%	$65.5K	23.0 (2008)
Belgium	54%	$53K	28.0 (2005)
The Netherlands	52%	$66.8K	30.9% (2007)
Finland	49%	$79.5K	26.8% (2008)
Canada	48%	$409.7K	32.1% (2005)
USA	44%	$400.3K	45.0% (2007)
Brazil	27.5%	$65.2K	51.9% (2012)

Source: OECD Tax Policy Centre (2013) and World Factbook (2013).

only 37% of them were girls. Under the political domination of Taliban rule that denied girls the right to education, from 1996–2001, parents also became reluctant to send their girls to school. Redistribution has the potential in theory of generating equalizing effects in the economy, but it is not a guarantee; access to public goods and services (like education) is co-determined by the political and socio-cultural environment. Finally, redistribution can also take place in selective ways, whereby certain groups of people or regions in a country are favored over others. In this way, politically favored groups can benefit from public goods and services, while others cannot.

Nevertheless, equity is not used as a prime indicator of economic performance. It will be interesting to see whether that changes in the near future.

7.3 Economic growth and beyond

In the previous section we have explained that efficiency, as a theoretical and practical concept, is limiting. Limiting because it does not capture other aspects of the economy that people deem important, and because of externalities. Efficiency is therefore not used as a measure to assess economic performance at the macro level. Instead, Gross Domestic Product (GDP) output is the dominant economic performance indicator. GDP is the market value of all goods and services that are produced within a country in a given period of time – commonly in a year. When an economy is performing well, GDP is increasing and we speak of economic growth. An economy is mal-performing when GDP is decreasing, which is a situation of economic shrinkage. Efficiency is subsumed by GDP growth, although not really measured by it. The underlying argument being that an economy can only grow when it produces a higher amount of goods and services than it uses or depreciates in the current production process over a specific period of time.

Box 7.5 Gross Domestic Product (GDP)

GDP is the market value of all final goods and services that are produced within a country in a given period of time – commonly in a year. The annual change in GDP, economic growth, is a dominant economic performance indicator.

Growth is measured by the periodical proportional change in GDP, as follows:

$$g = \Delta GDP = \frac{GDP_{t+1} - GDP_t}{GDP_t} \cdot 100\% \qquad (7.1)$$

Where g represents the periodical growth rate, Δ denotes change, and t is the time period considered. Whether or not economic growth translates in average per capita GDP growth depends on how fast the population of a country is growing. If the population growth rate (p) exceeds the economic growth rate (g), average per capita GDP will decrease. Only if economic growth exceeds population growth will average per capita GDP grow. The GDP per capita growth rate is the preferable measure for comparison between countries with differing population growth rates. Population growth is measured as follows:

$$p = Pop = \frac{Pop_{t+1} - Pop_t}{Pop_t} \cdot 100\% \qquad (7.2)$$

Whereby, p represents the population growth rate, and Pop denotes the number of persons in a population at a given time t. GDP per capita at a given time t is simply measured as:

$$GDP \ per \ capita = \frac{GDP_t}{Pop_t} \qquad (7.3)$$

So that, per capita economic growth is measured as:

$$g_{pc} = GDP_{pc} = \frac{\dfrac{GDP_{t+1}}{Pop_{t+1}} - \dfrac{GDP_t}{Pop_t}}{\dfrac{GDP_t}{Pop_t}} \cdot 100\% \qquad (7.4)$$

Growth can be achieved in multiple ways; for example, by means of market expansion, capital investments, increase in asset values, human capital advances, and/or technological innovation. The efficient use of resources is implied by economic growth, but not a pre-condition. For example, in the case of a monopoly producing at inefficient levels because it can set prices higher than in a competitive market, thus maximizing profits and leading to higher GDP. We therefore caution not to simply equate economic growth with efficiency.

Besides economic growth, other known performance indicators include the following:

- Unemployment rate – percentage share of the number of unemployed individuals of all individuals currently in the labor force.
- Inflation rate – percentage change in the overall price level of goods and service in an economy (normally the consumer price index)[2], over a given period of time.
- Economic stability – the absence in an economy of excessive fluctuations, with constant economic growth and a low and stable inflation rate.
- Income inequality – a distributional measure of income differences between individual persons or income groups, for example as measured by the Gini index.

These indicators shed light on the functioning of the paid economy exclusively. As such, these indicators have nothing to say about the unpaid economy, which constitutes the other side of the coin, as we learned in Chapter 2. What explains this prime attention to the paid economy?

Economic growth generates new resources. These resources can be used for making new investments in the (paid) factors of production, thus warranting more growth in the future when invested wisely. Growth predicates more growth, is the conventional argument. Growth achieved by private companies can also be used to pay dividend to shareholders. Factors of production are the inputs to the production process, including capital, labor and technology. However, economic opinions start to differ with what qualifies as 'factors of production'. In neoclassical growth theory, the factors of production include capital, labor and technology employed in the paid economy exclusively. However, and as feminist economists have pointed out in the past, these concepts nullify all capital, labor and technology employed in the unpaid economy, where household and voluntary goods and services are produced. This prime, but narrow attention to the paid economy is sometimes explained as a 'male-biased view'.[3] Furthermore, neoclassical growth theory excludes natural resources from the growth equation. The costs of extracting natural resources are included in conventional cost-benefit analysis, but not the cost of regenerating nature, or biodiversity loss. These omissions have led to blind spots in economic thinking about the potential sources of growth, which is problematic for a number of reasons.

- In economic theory, growth strategies directed at inputs of production in the paid economy are rationalized as being 'productive' and 'efficient', whereas growth strategies aimed at the inputs of production in the unpaid economy are dichotomized as costly and inefficient. The importance of unpaid work to economic performance has been undervalued and neglected as a result.
- As a result, investments in social and environmental resources are not seen as contributing to economic growth. Instead, social and environmental investments are seen to diminish growth rates because they are 'inefficient'.
- The above dichotomy has blocked innovative thinking about sources of growth beyond the paid economy, and the two-way interactions between the unpaid and paid economy from which new stimuli of economic growth and stability could originate.
- It has also biased economic reform measures, institution building and regulatory laws towards the paid economy, with secondary attention paid to the quality and security of human and natural capital of individuals, households, communities and social groups in the unpaid economy. As a result, their stewardship role over human and natural capital has been neglected.

7.4 The risk of empty growth

Economists, like Ian Goldin in 2009, predicted that future economic growth will come hand in hand with higher levels of inequality and systemic risk. More growth is then not necessarily better; the quality of growth also matters. Even 'empty growth' may take place, which augments the chances of uncontrollable risk and crisis to occur. Empty growth is an increase in GDP/capita that is not supported by real increases in human capital and asset values, but the result of speculative investments in assets, or excessive risk taking. High systemic risk and inequality may not only undermine future economic growth, but it may also impact negatively on human wellbeing.

Box 7.6 Empty growth

Empty growth is an increase in GDP/capita that is not backed-up by real increases in human capital and asset values, but the result of speculative investments in assets, or excessive risk taking. This was the case, for example, in the United States' 2007 subprime mortgage crisis that led to a global financial crisis. Low-quality subprime mortgages were given out to US citizens at rates increasing from 8 percent to 20 percent in four year's time. This economic bubble was created by a combination of lowering lending standards and adding higher-risk mortgage products. By the time the bubble burst, it was too late to realize how empty growth undermines economic stability and human wellbeing.

Source: Pouw (2011)

7.5 Towards a more inclusive output measurement

To fill in these blind spots it is important to make the aggregate contribution of unpaid household work and voluntary work visible and comparable to GDP at the macro-economic level. In this way we can see the relative importance of both sides of the economy. In Chapter 3 we described the importance of unpaid household work to the functioning of the paid economy. We also explained that the production of household goods and services has intrinsic value to the human wellbeing of household members. Within the framework of National Accounts it is possible to record the aggregate value of unpaid household work at the macro level of the economy in Satellite Accounts. The following indicators are used to assess the total market value of unpaid household work in the economy, what this amounts to per head of the household, and calculate its relative share of GDP.

• ***The total value of unpaid household work in the economy:***

Total value of unpaid household work $= TVUW_t = TUW_t \cdot MW_t$ (7.5)

Per capita value of unpaid household work $= \dfrac{TVUW_t}{Pop_t}$ (7.6)

Share of total value of unpaid household work in GDP

$$= \dfrac{TVUW_t}{GDP_t} \cdot 100\% \quad (7.7)$$

Whereby, $TVUW$ indicates the total value of unpaid household work produced at time t, TUW denotes the total time spent on unpaid household work, and MW the market wage equivalent of that time.

In Chapter 5 we described the economic value of voluntary work to economic growth and stability through social cohesion, human capital and income enhancement. Voluntary work also has intrinsic value to the human wellbeing of individual people and the communities or social groups from which they are members. The aggregate value of voluntary work can also be recorded at the macro level of the economy by means of Satellite Accounts. The following indicators are useful to assess the total market value of voluntary work in the economy, what this amounts to per head of the household, and calculate its relative share of GDP.

• ***The total value of voluntary work in the economy:***

Total value of voluntary work $= TVVW_t = TVW_t \cdot MW_t$ (7.8)

Per capita value of voluntary work $= \dfrac{TVVW_t}{Pop_t}$ (7.9)

Share of total value of voluntary work in GDP $= \dfrac{TVVW_t}{GDP_t} \cdot 100\%$

(7.10)

Whereby, *TVVW* indicates the total value of voluntary work produced at time *t*, *TVW* denotes the total time spent on voluntary work, and *MW* the market wage equivalent of that time.

Finally, for calculating the sum of unpaid household work and voluntary work together (i.e. all unpaid work in the economy) and compare its relative share to GDP, we use the following set of population and per capita indicators.

*   ***The total value of unpaid work in the economy:***

    Gross unpaid production = $GUP_t = TVUW_t + TVVW_t$ (7.11)

    Per capita unpaid production $= \dfrac{GUP_t}{Pop_t}$ (7.12)

    Share of GUP in GDP $= \dfrac{GUP_t}{GDP_t} \cdot 100\%$ (7.13)

We are now ready to assess the total values of goods and services produced in the unpaid and paid economy together. Remember that in Chapter 2 (Figure 7.1) we posited that the unpaid and paid economy form two sides of the same coin; together they make up the entire economy. In countries that keep Satellite Accounts of unpaid work (e.g. Canada, Australia, US, The Netherlands), the total value of unpaid work amounts to inbetween 40–50% of the GDP. Worldwide, if unpaid family workers in family business are counted in, the value of unpaid work rises to 60% of the GDP. These figures illustrate the importance of the unpaid and paid economy together. This brings us to the formulation of an all inclusive output measure of all goods and services produced in the economy (unpaid and paid economy), as follows:

*   ***Inclusive output measure:***

    Inclusive Output $(IO) = GUP + GDP$ (7.14)

The Inclusive Output (IO) measure calculated in this manner is likely to build in overlap between the value of unpaid and paid work. Part of the value of unpaid work is already factored in the price of paid goods and services. It is equally likely that many unpaid goods and services are not measured and unaccounted for in the Satellite

Accounts, so that their aggregate value is always underestimated. We assume there is truth in both claims, and that both issues will hopefully be resolved with economic measurement and accounting systems further gender-sensitizing and improving. For now, we sacrifice these imperfections to the benefits of having derived a more inclusive and gender-aware output measure for evaluating economic performance. The IO measure does more justice to women's and men's labor invested in production in the unpaid and paid economy. However, it does not resolve the problem of environmental externalities, since the IO does not value the depreciation of nature in the (unpaid or paid) production process. We will come back to this point when discussing alternative economic performance measures in Section 7.8 below.

7.6 The value of intangibles

In similar vein to the oversight of the value of unpaid work in measuring total output, the contribution of intangible assets has also been largely overlooked in the current system of national accounts. Intangible assets are identifiable non-monetary assets and include such immaterial things as social competencies, social cohesion, quality and efficiency of institutions, education and knowledge built up and shared within professions, households and communities/social groups of people.[4] Intangible assets have economic value because people expect to derive future benefits from them. Intangible assets are of increasing importance to the success of present-day economies, in the absence of which crises and conflicts would occur.[5] They are thus compounding factors to economic performance. This trend is caused by a growing share of economic production and trade consisting of private and public services that employ both tangible and intangible assets, and involve high levels of human capital that have been accumulated over a person's lifetime (for example, financial services, public health and education services).

Box 7.7 Intangible assets

> An intangible asset is an identifiable non-monetary asset without physical substance, from which future economic benefits are expected to flow. They are compounding factors to economic performance.

Source: International Accounting Standards Board (IAS38).

Intangible assets play a constitutive role in defining the parameters for the quality and modes of production. Under what physical and human conditions should production take place (e.g. safety standards, social protection)? What externalities of production and consumption do we accept as communities/groups of people, and which do we regard unacceptable? A great deal of intangible assets is produced at the interface of, and within, the unpaid and paid economy. Intangible assets are often produced by co-creation. The dividing line between the unpaid and paid economy then becomes blurred. This is one reason why intangible assets do not feature in national accounts, the other reason being the difficulty of their measurement. In the following section we will see how intangible assets are included in economic indicators that aim to measure economic performance toward delivering social and environmental value to people in the economy.

7.7 The value of natural resources

For many years economic growth models have included a price for labour (wage) and capital (rent), but not for nature. Yet, nature holds both intrinsic and instrumental value for economic performance and human wellbeing. The depletion of natural resources and of biodiversity undermines present human wellbeing, future growth and development. Environmental depletion also has global impacts, which makes it a global problem. Impacts of environmental depletion are typically unequally distributed. People who are dependent on natural resources for the largest share of their livelihood experience the negative impacts of natural degradation and environmental pollution the most. However, we cannot forget that ultimately our entire society is embedded within and dependent upon our natural environment – see also Figure 4 in Chapter 3.

The costs of extracting natural resources from nature *are* included as operational costs of production; however, natural capital itself is commonly not valued in standard economic growth models, or in economic cost-benefit analysis. Ecological economists and green growth economists have stressed the importance of including the value of nature in economic growth models,[6] otherwise there is a tendency for over usage and wasteful practises. But natural capital has remained under-/non-priced and as a result, the depreciation of nature is not counted. Putting a price on nature will make their absolute and relative scarcity visible. It does not mean all natural capital becomes a market commodity. Current economic growth patterns are fundamentally unsustainable from this point of view.

Johan Rockström (2009) and his team at the Stockholm Resilience Centre defined nine planetary boundaries to ecosystems that define the safe operating levels of the economy. The boundaries set the dividing line between sustainable and unsustainable ecological system level – beyond the boundary the system changes into a different state and may lead to irreversible biodiversity loss. At the time of writing this book, 2017, three of the nine boundaries have already transgressed (see Table 7.2): climate change, rate of biodiversity loss, and nitrogen cycle. Given this shrinking global ecospace, and in view of present day unsustainable consumption and production patterns, renders the question even more pertinent, 'How to allocate resources?'. Particularly, allocating resources in an equitable manner, is becoming one of the most critical questions. Stern (2006)

Molly Cato-Scott (2012) defines the green economy as one that results in improved human wellbeing and social equity, while significantly reducing environmental risks and ecological scarcities. In the neoliberal economic growth discourse there is a fallacy of trade-off between economic growth and the environment – instead it is a *loop*: investing in the green economy will generate more benefits than costs. According to a green economy perspective, cleaner growth is possible by using the following instruments.

Box 7.8 The green economy

> The green economy is an economy that results in improved human wellbeing and social equity, while significantly reducing environmental risks and ecological scarcities.

Source: Cato-Scott (2012)

First of all, investments in nature are necessary to give nature a chance to regenerate itself. Therefore, the use of natural resources needs to be taxed. This tax income can be used to invest in the regeneration and preservation of nature. Second, nature holds intrinsic value to communities/social groups, but not all natural capitals can be priced. Nevertheless, this can be protected and maintained by means of letting people pay for its usage, or by means of granted support by the government or private funds if people agree that this is important. Third, a common-pool natural resource base may constitute a livelihood base for specific communities/social groups. Restricted usage of common-pool resources can be agreed upon by defining user rights. Alternatively, communities/social groups depending on common-pool resources can be compensated for external usage. Feminist scholars have pointed to women's relatively close relationship to nature, which is encompassed in their gender roles as food providers and caretakers of the family. Because of this, women may hold specific knowledge on sustainable resource use and preservation

Table 7.2 The nine planetary boundaries

Earth system process	Parameters	Proposed boundary	Current status	Pre-industrial boundary
Climate change	**(1) Atmospheric carbon dioxide concentration (parts per million by volume)**	**350**	**387**	**280**
	(2) Change in radioactive forcing (watts per metre squared)	**1**	**1.5**	**0**
Rate of biodiversity loss	**Extinction rate (number of species per million species per year)**	**10**	**100**	**0.1-1**
Nitrogen cycle (part of a boundary with the phosphorus cycle)	**Amount of N_2 removed from the atmosphere for human use (millions of tonnes per year)**	**35**	**121**	**0**
Phosphorus cycle (part of a boundary with the nitrogen cycle)	Quantity of P flowing into the ocean (millions of tonnes per year)	11	8.5-9.5	-1
Stratospheric ozone depletion	Concentration of ozone (Dobson unit)	276	283	290

Earth-system process	Parameter			
Ocean acidification	Global mean saturation state of aragonite in ocean surface water	2.75	2.83	2.90
Global fresh water use	Consumption of freshwater by humans (km³ per year)	4,000	2,600	415
Change in land use	Percentage of global land cover converted to cropland	15	11.7	Low
Atmospheric aerosol loading	Overall particulate concentration in the atmosphere, on a regional basis	To be determined		
Chemical pollution	For example, amount emitted to, or concentration of persistent organic pollutants, plastics, endocrine disrupters, heavy metals and nuclear waste in the global environment, or the effects on ecosystem and functioning of Earth system thereof	To be determined		

Source: From Rockström, J. et al., *Ecology and society*, *14*, 2, 1033–1049, 2009.
Note: boundaries in bold have been transgressed.

that is often not well-documented, shared or upscaled. Women's knowledge is therefore rarely the starting point of agricultural extension or environmental training and development interventions, which cᵒnstitutes a missed opportunity for policy makers and practitioners on the ground.

7.8 Measuring social progress and wellbeing

World-wide initiatives are taken to develop more encompassing macro indices of social progress and wellbeing beyond GDP growth. Intangible assets feature prominently in such indices. The examples presented below are all examples of composite indices. A composite index is constructed by grouping a number of indicators or actors together in a standardized way, providing a comprehensive statistical measure of an overall phenomenon. A composite index may consist of a set of quantitative and qualitative variables together. Qualitative variables are then transformed into numerical scores using a Likert scale, so that an overall score can be computed. Alternatively, the relative weight of a series of dependent variables can be assessed in relation to the independent variable through multiple regression analysis.

Box 7.9 Composite index

A composite index is constructed by grouping a number of indicators or actors together in a standardized way, providing a comprehensive statistical measure of an overall phenomenon.

The following four composite indices will be explained below:[7]

1   Quality of Life Index
2   Better Life Index
3   Social Progress Index
4   Index of Sustainable Economic Welfare

7.8.1 Quality of life index

Since 2005, The Economist's Intelligence Unit computes an annual Quality of Life index from the Gallup Poll survey[8], based on people's subjective evaluation of the quality of life in 111 countries on a scale from 1 to 10. The quality of life score is related to ten explanatory factors, whose relative weights are assigned through a multiple regression procedure. These ten factors include quantitative indicators that are assessed using either objective or subjective measures: (i) material wellbeing (GDP per capita); (ii) life expectancy at birth; (iii) family life (divorce rates); (iv) state of political freedoms (subjective evaluations of political and civic freedoms); (v) job security (unemployment rate); (vi) climate (average deviation of minimum and maximum monthly temperatures from 14°C; and the number of months/year with rainfall <30 mm.); (vii) personal security (homicide rates; and risk from crime and terrorism); (viii) community life (membership in social organizations); (ix) governance (corruption); and (x) gender equality (women's share of seats in parliament).

7.8.2 Better life index

The OECD in 2011 developed the Better Life Index as way of measuring wellbeing at the national level in 36 countries (counting 2013). Compared to GDP growth, the Better Life Index is seen by its designers to better capture the different elements of social welfare and the trade offs between them.[9] The index measures life satisfactions in 11 wellbeing domains, relating the subjective assessments to one or more objective indicators: (i) housing (number of rooms/person; dwellings with basic facilities; housing expenditures); (ii) income (household net adjusted disposable income; household financial wealth); (iii) jobs (employment rate; long-term unemployment rate; average earnings; job security); (iv) community (helping others; social support network); (v) education (educational attainment; years in education; students' skills); (vi) environment (air pollution; water quality); (vii) civic engagement (voter turnout; consultation on rule-making); (viii) health (life expectancy; self-reported health); (ix) life satisfaction (life satisfaction as a whole); (x) safety (assault rate; homicide rate); (xi) work-life-balance (employees working long hours; time spent on leisure and personal care).

7.8.3 Social progress index

The Social Progress Index was first introduced in 2013, assessing social progress in 132 countries (counting 2014). The Social Progress Index (SPI) follows-up on the recommendation of the 2009 Sarkozy report on 'Measuring Economic Performance and Social Progress'[10], to evaluate social progress by means of a more encompassing measure than GDP growth. The SPI is also a composite index that aims to capture the wellbeing outcomes in the following three dimensions: (i) Basic Human Needs; (ii) Foundations of Wellbeing; and (iii) Opportunity (see Figure 7.1). Within each dimension, four components are measured by 54 distinct indicators.[11] These contain social and environmental variables, but no income or economic output-related variables. As such, the SPI can be used as a complement to the GDP measure to assess economic performance in multiple life domains. The selection of social and environmental components within each dimension illustrates, once again,

Figure 7.1 The Social Progress Index (SPI).
Source: Porter and Stern (2014)

that indicators such as these are also social constructs. Not each and every society in the world would subscribe to the importance of 'Personal Rights' or 'Access to Advanced Education' for men and women alike.

7.8.4 Index of sustainable economic welfare

The Index of Sustainable Economic Welfare (ISEW) was originally designed in 1989 by ecological-economist Herman Daly and theologian, philosopher and environmentalist John B. Cobb, and his son Christopher Cobb.[12] The ISEW is computed according to the same principles as GDP, by adding-up and subtracting monetary values out of which a single number arises:

ISEW = personal consumption
+ services from household labor
+ public non-defensive expenditures
+ capital formation
– private defensive expenditures
– costs of environmental degradation
– depreciation of natural capital

The ISEW recognizes the value of unpaid household labor services and the costs of environmental degradation and depreciation of natural capital. If the social and environmental costs outweigh the economic benefits, this means economic growth does not lead to the enhancement of welfare (as according to Daly's and Cobb's definition of welfare). Later versions of the ISEW index include particular additions and breakdowns of costs leading to the construction of the related Genuine Progress Indicator (GPI). The GPI is informed also by the work of economist John Hicks[13] and his work on sustainable income – meaning the maximum amount a person or economy can consume in one period without diminishing consumption in the next period.

The GPI indicator is based on the concept of sustainable income, presented by economist John Hicks (1939). The sustainable income is the maximum amount a person or an economy can consume during one period without decreasing his or her consumption during the next period. Unsustainable income then means consumption whereby capital drawdown takes place. In the same manner, the GPI assesses the level of welfare by taking into account the ability to maintain welfare on at least the same level in the future (see Box 7.10).

Box 7.10 The components of GPI

+ Personal consumption weighted by income distribution index
+ Value of household work and parenting
+ Value of higher education
+ Value of volunteer work
+ Services of consumer durables
+ Services of highways and streets
− Cost of crime
− Loss of leisure time
− Cost of unemployment
− Cost of consumer durables
− Cost of commuting
− Cost of household pollution abatement
− Cost of automobile accidents
− Cost of water pollution
− Cost of air pollution
− Cost of noise pollution
− Loss of wetlands
− Loss of farmland
−/+ Loss of forest area and damage from logging roads
− Depletion of nonrenewable energy resources
− Carbon dioxide emissions damage
− Cost of ozone depletion
+/− Net capital investment
+/− Net foreign borrowing
= GPI

The economic performance debate forms the stepping stone for a gender-aware perspective on the macro-economy that will be the focus of Volume II. The essence of this debate is the quality of growth in terms of social relations, sustainability and voice and empowerment, matters as a distinctive factor of economic performance. McGregor and Pouw (2016). Growth is a means to an end, rather than the end in itself. A gender-aware perspective on the micro economy would certainly benefit from such a broadening conception of economic performance, as it provides multiple angles for considering gender as an ex-ante concern, rather than as ex-post.

7.9 Learning points

- Economic performance is the assessment of an economy in relation to how it functions and what outcomes it produces to the people who constitute the economy, and the environment in which it is embedded.
- An economic externality is a cost or benefit that affects people in society or the environment that did not choose to incur that cost or benefit.
- Efficiency broadly refers to the ability to utilize resources without wasting resources.
- Equity, or economic equality refers to a sense of 'fairness' in economic opportunities and/or outcomes.
- Gross Domestic Product (GDP) is the market value of all final goods and services that are produced within a country in a given period of time – commonly in a year. The annual change in GDP, economic growth, is a dominant economic performance indicator.
- An intangible asset is an identifiable non-monetary asset without physical substance, from which future economic benefits are expected to flow. They are compounding factors to economic performance.
- The green economy is an economy that results in improved human wellbeing and social equity, while significantly reducing environmental risks and ecological scarcities.
- New indexes try to evaluate economic performance beyond the GDP measure in a more comprehensive manner.

7.10 Assignments and discussion points

Discussion point 1 – How do economies perform? (15–20 minutes)
Ask each pair of two participants to think about the *key functions* of the economy. After having written down some key functions, invite two participants to put these functions in a drawing of the economy on the board. Discuss what/who is at the centre of the economy, what are its key functions, and when is an economy performing well. Open the floor for discussion and try to agree on a short-list of key functions.

Assignment 1 – Calculating the Value of Unpaid Labour (15 minutes)
Try to estimate how many hours you spend on various tasks of unpaid household work per week on average (including shopping, cooking, cleaning, caring tasks, etc.). Look up the hourly minimum wage for someone of your age and write down this value. Calculate with the help of equation (6.5) what the weekly market value equivalent is of your unpaid work. How does that compare to your total income (if any)? Use equation (6.7) to compute your share of unpaid work value out of total income. If this share exceeds 100 percent, what does this mean? If this share is lower than 100 percent, what does this mean? Discuss the advantages and disadvantages of an inclusive output measure of economic output from a gender-aware perspective?

Discussion point 2 – Intangible Assets (10 minutes)
Ask the group of participants to name five examples of intangible assets in the economy. List them on a board. Discuss how the significance of intangible assets has increased in recent decades, in a more globalized economy?

Discussion point 3 – Valuing Nature (10 minutes)
In 2015, global investments in renewable energy rose by 5 percent to 285.9 billion US$. Discuss with the group how this contributes to economic performance in broad terms.

Notes

1 See Thomas Piketty's (2013) historical analysis of income and wealth inequality in his book on *Capital in the Twenty-First Century*.
2 The consumer price index (CPI) measures all changes in the price level of a basket of consumer goods and services bought by households in the market. The CPI is commonly measured by a country's statistical bureau.
3 For example, see Marianne Ferber and Julie Nelson's (eds.) (1993) Be*yond Economic Man. Feminist Theory and Economics*, in which they postulate that economic theories and methods have suffered from an inherent masculine bias.
4 See also Jean-Paul Fitoussi and Khalid Malik's (2012) exposition on the value of intangible assets and other social goods for capabiliy development and sustainability in their occasional paper for UNDP on 'Choices, Capabilities and Sustainability'.
5 The growing importance of intangibles in present-day economies was one of the main points stressed in the "Sarkozy report" of 2009, written by Joseph Stiglitz, Amartya Sen and Jean-Paul Fittousi.
6 The OECD has developed one way in which natural capital can be included into an environmental-economic growth model. First, by including energy use into the model and putting a price on usage. Second, by including the value-added of natural resources, broken down in physical capital and imposing costs of extraction from reserves and deriving rents. How to exactly include

natural capital into economic models is subject to much debate. In Volume II on the Macroeconomy, we will engage in further depth with this topic from a gender-aware perspective.

7 It should be noted that this is not an exhaustive list. New initiatives to design more comprehensive indexes keep coming up.

8 The Gallup World Poll survey consists of global and region-specific questions, covering topics such as: law and order, food and shelter, institutions and infrastructure, good jobs, wellbeing, and brain gain. The US Gallup Poll surveys citizens in 160 countries on a continuous basis, representing more than 98% of the world's adult population. See: http://en.wikipedia.org/wiki/Gallup_Poll#Gallup_Poll.

9 See the background documents on the OECD Better Life Index on-line at: http://www.oecdbetterlifeindex.org/blog/is-gdp-still-useful.htm.

10 The Social Progress Index was designed by Douglas North, Amartya Sen and Joseph Stiglitz, the latter two whom were authors of the Sarkozy report (together with Jean-Paul Fitoussi).

11 These include: for (i) Basic Human Needs: (i.1) Nutrition and basic medical health care: undernourishment, depth of food deficit, maternal mortality rate, stillbirth rate, child mortality rate, death from infectious diseases; (i.2) Water and sanitation: access to piped water, rural versus urban access to improved water source, access to improved sanitation facilities; (i.3) Shelter: availability of affordable housing, access to electricity, quality of electricity supply, indoor air pollution attributable deaths; (i.4) Personal safety: homicide rate, level of violent crime, perceived criminality, political terror, traffic deaths; (ii) Foundations of Wellbeing: (ii.1) Access to basic knowledge: adult literacy rate, primary school enrolment, lower secondary school enrolment, upper secondary school enrolment, gender parity in secondary enrolment; (ii.2) Access to information and communications: mobile telephone subscriptions, internet users, Press Freedom Index; (ii.3) Health and Wellness: life expectancy, non-communicable disease deaths between 30 and 70, obesity rate, outdoor air pollution attributable deaths, suicide rate; (ii.4) Ecosystem sustainability: greenhouse gas emissions, water withdrawals as a percent of resources, biodiversity and habitat; (iii) Opportunity: (iii.1) Personal rights: political rights, freedom of speech, freedom of assembly/association, freedom of movement, private property rights; (iii.2) Personal freedom and choice: freedom over life choices, freedom of religion, modern slavery/human trafficking/child marriage, satisfied demand for contraception, corruption; (iii.3) Tolerance and inclusion: women treated with respect, tolerance for immigrants, tolerance for homosexuals, discrimination and violence against minorities, religious tolerance, community safety net; (iii.4): Access to advanced education: years of tertiary schooling, women's average years in school, inequality in the attainment of education, number of globally ranked universities. Source: Social Progress Imperative (2014).

12 See also: Cobb and Daly's book (1989) on *For the Common Good: Redirecting the Economy Toward Community, Environment, and a Sustainable Future*.

13 John Hicks (1904) was a British economist who became known for his works on equilibrium theory and welfare economics. He was awarded the Nobel Prize, together with Kenneth Arrow in 1973. His ideas on sustainable income are described in his 1939 book on *Value and Capital: An Inquiry into Some Fundamental Principles of Economic Theory*.

References and suggested further reading

Cato, M. S. (2012). Green economics: Putting the planet and politics back into economics. *Cambridge Journal of Economics*, 36 (5), 1033–1049.

Daly, H. and Cobb J.B.Jr (1989). *For the Common Good: Redirecting the Economy Toward Community, Environment, and a Sustainable Future*. Boston, MA: Beacon Press.

Ferber, M. and Nelson J. (eds.) (1993) Beyond Economic Man Feminist Theory and Economics, Chicago: The University of Chicago Press.

Goldin, I. (2009). Ian Goldin: Navigating Our Global Future. TED Talk.

Hicks, J.R. (1939) *Value and Capital: An Inquiry into Some Fundamental Principles of Economic Theory*. Oxford, UK: Clarendon Press.

McGregor, A.J. and Pouw N.R.M. (2016) Towards an Economics of Wellbeing. *Cambridge Journal of Economics*. doi:10.1093/cje/bew044.

OECD Tax Policy Centre (2013). *Tax Policy Analysis 2013*. Accessible on-line: http://www.oecd.org/ctp/tax-policy/

O'Laughlin, B. and Pouw N. (2004) Poverty and the quality of life: Capabilities and livelihoods. Study Guide Module, 1.

Piketty, T. (2013). *Capital in the Twenty-First Century*. Cambridge, London: The Bellknapp Press of Harvard University Press.

Porter, M.E. and Stern S. with Green M. (2014) *The Social Progress Index 2014*. Washington, DC: Social Progress Imperative.

Pouw, N. R. M. (2011). When growth is empty: towards an inclusive economics. The Broker, 25. Amsterdam: The Broker.

Rockström, J., Steffen, W., Noone, K., Persson, Å., Chapin III, F. S., Lambin, E.. et al (2009). Planetary boundaries: Exploring the safe operating space for humanity. *Ecology and society*, 14 (2), 1033–1049.

Social Progress Imperative (2014) . *Social Progress Index*. Website last visited 28 May 2014: http://www.socialprogressimperative.org/data/spi

Stern, N. (2006). *Economics of Climate Change*.

Stiglitz, J., Sen. A.K. and Fitoussi J.P. (2009) *Measuring Economic Performance and Social Progress*. Paris: Report by the Commission on Commission on the Measurement of Economic Performance and Social Progress.

Index